MEDIAEVAL SOURCES IN TRANSLATION

15

MASTER ECKHART

PARISIAN QUESTIONS AND PROLOGUES

Translated with an Introduction and Notes

by

ARMAND A. MAURER, C.S.B.

PONTIFICAL INSTITUTE OF MEDIAEVAL STUDIES
TORONTO, CANADA
1974

This book has been reprinted with the help
of a grant from the De Rancé Foundation.

CATALOGUING DATA [REVISED]

Eckhart, Meister, d. 1327
Parisian questions and prologues / Master Eckhart ; translated with an introd. and notes by Armand A. Maurer — Toronto : Pontifical Institute of Mediaeval Studies, 1974.

(Mediaeval sources in translation ; 15 ISSN 0316-0874)
123 p. ; 20 cm.
Bibliography: p. [115]-117.
Includes index.
ISBN 0-88844-264-5

1. God – Adresses, essays, lectures. I. Maurer, Armand Augustine 1915- II. Pontifical Institute of Mediaeval Studies. III. Title. IV. Series.

BT100.E27 1974 231

Pontifical Institute of Mediaeval Studies
59 Queen's Park Crescent East
Toronto, Ontario, Canada M5S 2C4

PRINTED BY UNIVERSA, WETTEREN, BELGIUM

TABLE OF CONTENTS

INTRODUCTION

Life and Works

Eckhart has long been an enigma to historians of western thought. In his own day he was accused of heresy and shortly after his death twenty-eight of his theses were condemned as unorthodox. Some contemporaries regarded him as a sympathizer with the "Brethren of the Free Spirit," who were harshly persecuted for their pantheistic and antinomian doctrines.[1] He has been considered the father of German mysticism, the enemy of Christian orthodoxy, the persecuted champion of truths higher than Christianity, a spokesman for the enlightenment, and even a forerunner of Luther and German idealism.[2] At the same time it has been recognized that he inspired, and was held in reverence by, such thoroughly orthodox spiritual writers as Tauler, Ruysbroeck, Suso, and Nicholas of Cusa. Today, M. D. Knowles can write that "of his radical traditionalism and orthodoxy there is no longer any doubt."[3]

1 See R. E. Lerner, *The Heresy of the Free Spirit in the Later Middle Ages* (Berkeley, Los Angeles, London, 1972), p. 2. Josef Koch believed that Eckhart knew *The Mirror of Simple Souls* by Marguerite Porete, the leader of the Free Spirit movement. Unfortunately Koch's death prevented him from pursuing this topic. See *op. cit.*, p. 183. On Marguerite Porete, see E. Colledge, "Liberty of Spirit: 'The Mirror of Simple Souls'," *Theology of Renewal* (Toronto, 1968), II, 100-117.

2 For a good bibliography of German mysticism, see F. W. Wentzlaff-Eggebert, *Deutsche Mystik zwischen Mittelalter und Neuzeit*, 2nd ed. (Tübingen, 1947). For Eckhart's relations to German mysticism, see J. M. Clark, *The Great German Mystics, Eckhart, Tauler and Suso* (Oxford, 1949); J. Ancelet-Hustache, *Master Eckhart and the Rhineland Mystics*, transl. by Hilda Graef (New York, 1957). E. von Bracken has recently assessed Eckhart in relation to modern thought: *Meister Eckhart: Legende und Wirklichkeit* (Meisenheim an Glan, 1972).

3 M. D. Knowles, "Denifle and Ehrle," *History* LIV (1969), 4.

His doctrine is sometimes characterized as basically Thomistic, and sometimes as opposed to Thomism. It is still debated "whether Eckhart was a mystic using scholastic terminology, or a theologian adopting a Neoplatonic outlook."[4] So many divergent strains of doctrine have been found in his writings that E. Gilson could write: "The difficulty is not to find a good interpretation of Master Eckhart, but rather to choose between so many consistent interpretations, based upon unimpeachable texts, and yet differing among themselves to the point of sometimes being contradictory."[5]

In the face of this enigma the only recourse for the student of Eckhart's thought is the thorough reading of all his extant works against their contemporary background and seen in the light of their sources. Certainly, in this connection the surviving sermon notes and German spiritual treatises are important, but more essential still are Eckhart's Latin writings, some of which are here translated into English for the first time. These show, better than what little of his spiritual works has survived, the brilliance of his thought and the clarity of his expression, when he was arguing among the learned and not addressing more popular gatherings where, as his career advanced, he seems to have been encouraged in his unfortunate propensity for audacious and scandalous paradox.[6]

Many of the events of Eckhart's life, especially of his early years, are shrouded in legend; few dates are known with cer-

4 *Ibid.*

5 E. Gilson, Préface to V. Lossky, *Théologie négative et connaissance de Dieu chez Maître Eckhart* (Paris, 1960), p. 9.

6 Examples may be found among his condemned theses, in J. Ancelet-Hustache, *op. cit.*, pp. 133-138.

tainty.[7] He was born about 1260 in one of two towns named Hochheim in Thuringia. He entered the Dominican Order while a boy and made his novitiate and early studies at Erfurt. In 1277 he was a student of arts at Paris, and before 1280 he began to study theology at the Dominican *studium generale* in Cologne, where the memory of its founder, St. Albert the Great, was still revered. Eckhart's brilliance as a pupil pointed him to higher studies, and in 1293-1294 he was in Paris, lecturing on the *Sentences* of Peter Lombard and preparing for his master's degree in theology. At Paris his home was the Dominican house of Saint Jacques, where St. Thomas Aquinas had lived more than a generation before. Shortly afterward Eckhart was named prior of the Dominican house at Erfurt and vicar general of Thuringia. In 1302 he graduated as master in sacred theology, and ever after he was called "Master Eckhart" as a mark of respect.

About 1303 Eckhart was named provincial of the Dominican province of Saxony, and he continued in this post until 1311. In that year the General Chapter of Naples relieved him of this duty and he was again sent to Paris to teach theology. From 1313 to 1323 he was professor of theology at Strasbourg. During this period he was very popular as a preacher and spiritual director for both religious men and women and layfolk.

In 1326 the archbishop of Cologne, Henry of Virneburg, called him before the tribunal of the Inquisition as suspect of heresy. Unsatisfied with the procedure and competence of the

7 For Eckhart's life, see H. S. Denifle, "Meister Eckeharts lateinische Schriften, und die Grundanschauung seiner Lehre," *Archiv für Literatur und Kirchengeschichte des Mittelalters* (Berlin, Freiburg im Breisgau), II (1886), 417-615; J. Koch, "Kritische Studien zum Leben Meister Eckharts," *Arch. Fr. Praed.* 29 (1959), 5-51; 30 (1960), 5-52; J. Ancelet-Hustache, *op. cit.*, pp. 23-44; J. M. Clark, *Meister Eckhart. An Introduction to the Study of his Works with an Anthology of his Sermons* (London, Paris, 1957), pp. 11-25.

tribunal, Eckhart appealed directly to the pope. On February 13, 1327, in the Dominican church in Cologne, he publicly answered the charges against him. In a lengthy report he attempted to clear himself by explaining the meaning of his statements which had been criticized by his accusers. He then set out for Avignon to plead his case personally with the pope. He died before the conclusion of his trial, in 1327 or the beginning of 1328. Shortly before his death he made a profession of faith, retracting anything he had written or said contrary to the faith or causing heresy in others. On March 27, 1329, Pope John XXII condemned 28 propositions taken from his works and sermons; 17 he declared to be erroneous or tainted with heresy, the other 11 he described as "offensive, very temerarious and suspect of heresy, though, with many explanations and additions they might take on, or have, a Catholic sense."

Eckhart left both German and Latin writings. The German works comprise numerous sermons and several spiritual treatises. The Latin works include a Commentary on the *Sentences,* of which only the Introduction has survived;[8] several Disputed Questions; a sermon on St. Augustine; part of a treatise on the Pater Noster; many commentaries on Scripture, of which two on Genesis, one on Exodus, Ecclesiasticus, Wisdom, and the Gospel according to John have come down to us; Eckhart's Defense against his accusers; and Prologues to the *Opus Tripartitum.*

Of all these works, the Opus Tripartitum was to be his masterpiece. As the title indicates, it was designed on a grand scale to contain three parts: *Opus Propositionum,* in which a thousand or

8 J. Koch believed he might have found a manuscript of this work in Ms. Bruges, Bibliothèque de la Ville 491. See his article "Zur Analogielehre Meister Eckharts," *Mélanges offerts à Etienne Gilson* (Toronto, Paris, 1959), p. 331, n. 10.

more propositions were to be stated, explained, and defended; *Opus Quaestionum,* containing questions arranged according to the order of St. Thomas' *Summa*; and *Opus Expositionum*, divided into two parts, the first containing commentaries on Scripture and the second sermons (*Opus Sermonum*). This elaborate work was likely begun in Eckhart's maturity, probably after 1314, and it occupied him until the closing years of his life. Whether he completed it is not known. In any case only the General Prologue and the Prologues to the *Opus Propositionum* and *Opus Expositionum* have come down to us. According to Nicholas of Cusa, Eckhart produced many Disputed Questions, all of which were undoubtedly to enter into the *Opus Quaestionum*. Regrettably only a few disputed at Paris have survived. The extant commentaries were no doubt among those that were to be gathered together in the *Opus Expositionum*. The Latin sermons that survive do not constitute the second part of this work, the *Opus Sermonum*; they are only sermon notes.

The present book is a translation of the Parisian Disputed Questions and Prologues to the *Opus Tripartitum*. The first two Questions are records of disputations conducted by Eckhart during the scholastic year 1302-1303, when he was regent master in the Dominican chair of theology for foreigners (non-Parisians) at Paris. The same year the Franciscan Gonsalvo of Spain held the Franciscan chair as regent master.[9] The third Disputed Question here translated records a disputation between Gonsalvo and Eckhart on the relative superiority of the intellect and will. The fourth and fifth Questions, which treat of

9 Gonsalvus Hispanus was born in the province of Galicia, Spain, and died in 1313. He has been confused with another Franciscan, Gonsalvus de Vallebona or Balboa. See article on Gonsalvus, with bibliography, by G. Gál in *New Catholic Encyclopedia*, VI, pp. 608-609.

problems in the philosophy of nature, though in a theological context, date from Eckhart's second Parisian period, between 1311 and 1314.

These writings reveal the mind of a powerful and original speculative theologian and metaphysician. Eckhart draws upon the wisdom of the past: philosophers from Parmenides to Avicenna, theologians from Augustine to Thomas Aquinas; Scripture was the enduring font of his speculation. But everything he touched came into new focus and sprang into new life in his hands. He knew well that his listeners and readers would be shocked by some of his sayings, but he defended novelty and boldness of expression as a valuable stimulant to the mind in its progression toward truth. He shows a particular fondness for his confrère Thomas Aquinas, who himself was no stranger to revolutionary teachings and like Eckhart came under ecclesiastical censure; but he was not a man to repeat another's words without rethinking and redefining them in his own way. His personal perspective, and his relations to his predecessors, will be clarified if we analyze the translated Questions and Prologues.

Brief Analysis of the Texts

1. *The Parisian Questions.*

The first Parisian Question concerns the identity of existence and knowing in God; more basically it addresses itself to the metaphysical problem of the meaning of existence (*esse*) and its relation to such perfections as living and knowing.[10]

10 In translating Eckhart's texts *esse* has been regularly rendered 'existence' and *ens* 'being'. For the justification of this, see below, p. 29.

Eckhart defends the position that in God existence and knowing are identical in reality and perhaps even in our thought about them (*ratione*). He takes the same stand in his commentaries on Scripture, though in these works he does not qualify it with the cautious 'perhaps'. Verbally at least this contradicts Thomas Aquinas, who wrote in his *Summa*: "In God to be and to know are one and the same thing, differing only in our manner of understanding them (*secundum intelligentiae rationem*)."[11] According to Aquinas we can attribute a plurality of perfections to God without compromising his real unity; and yet the plurality of the divine names is also on the side of God himself, at least in the sense that "there is something in God corresponding to all these concepts, namely his complete and absolute perfection, by reason of which all these names signifying these concepts can be truly and properly predicated of him."[12]

Eckhart does not seem to have been pleased with this way of putting the matter, for it appeared to him to compromise the divine unity, which was always uppermost in his mind. He agreed with Aquinas that we can form many concepts of God which are not synonymous in meaning, but he emphasized that this posits no distinction in God himself *or even in our thought about him,* for "he who sees duality or distinction does not see God."[13] In God himself no distinction can be or even be thought. In Eckhart's view the Jewish theologian Maimonides summed this up neatly in his statement: "God is one in every

11 St. Thomas, *Summa Theol.* I, 26, 2.

12 St. Thomas, *In I Sent.* d. 2, q. 1, a. 3; ed. Mandonnet (Paris, 1929), I, p. 71.

13 *Expositio libri Exodi*, c. 15, v. 3; *Meister Eckhart, Die lateinischen Werke*, ed. Stuttgart, II, p. 65. Henceforth cited as *LW*. "It is clear that these [divine] names are not synonyms because they signify different *rationes* or conceptions of our intellect." *Ibid.* p. 66.

way and according to all reasoning (*secundum omnem rationem*)."[14] Eckhart's accusers, for their part, seem to have thought that this interpretation of the divine unity makes God completely unknowable and (against the background of Maimonides) to imply a denial of the Trinity, and they placed it in the list of his condemned propositions.[15] Eckhart himself saw no difficulty in reconciling this with orthodox Christian doctrine: in his Defense he protests that it is in harmony with Scripture, the saints and doctors of the Church.[16]

This initial divergence of Eckhart from Aquinas deepens as we proceed. Defending the identity of existence and knowing in God, Eckhart first appeals to six arguments in Aquinas' *Contra Gentiles* and *Summa.*[17] All of these are based on the simplicity and primacy of the divine being. He then presents another drawn from Aquinas' *De Ente et Essentia.*[18] In this work St. Thomas contends that God is pure *Esse* or Act of existing, and as such he possesses all perfections. In perfect simplicity the *Esse* that is God embraces every other perfection. Whatever God is or does, he is and does in virtue of his simple *Esse.* In this perspective, *esse* is the ground of all the divine perfections and operations; to live, to know, to act in any way — such as

14 *Ibid.* See Maimonides, *Dux seu Director Dubitantium aut Perplexorum*, I, c. 50 (Leipzig, 1522), fol. 18v. *The Guide of the Perplexed*, trans. by S. Pines (Chicago, 1963), p. 113.

15 G. Théry, "Edition critique des pièces relatives au procès d'Eckhart," *Archives d'histoire doctrinale et littéraire du moyen âge*, I (1926), p. 175, n. 10.

16 *Op. cit.*, p. 195, n. 10. "As for the tenth, when it says: 'God is one in all ways, according to all reasoning, etc.' it must be admitted that this is true as it stands and is in harmony with the Scripture of the canon, of the saints, and of the teachers." See R. B. Blakney, *Meister Eckhart, A Modern Translation* (New York, London, 1941), p. 265, n. 10.

17 St. Thomas, *Contra Gentiles*, I, c. 45; *Summa Theol.* I, 14, 4.

18 St. Thomas, *De Ente et Essentia*, 5; ed. Roland-Gosselin (Paris, 1926), pp. 38-39; trans. A. Maurer (Toronto, 1968), pp. 61-62, n. 3.

creating or begetting the Son — is nothing over and above his simple being. Hence in God existence (*esse*) and knowing are identical, existence being the ground and basis of his knowing.

This argument presupposes the primacy and excellence of being with respect to knowing. Eckhart was certainly aware that this was the doctrine of Aquinas; and he must have known that Duns Scotus also defended the primacy in God of being over knowledge, for in the very year that Eckhart was disputing this question at Paris (1302) the Subtle Doctor was in that city upholding this position in his commentary on the *Sentences*.[19]

Eckhart acknowledges that this was once his own teaching, but he explains that he has now changed his mind regarding the relation between being and knowing in God. He no longer believes that God knows because he exists, but that he exists because he knows. Knowing, in short, is the ground of being, and not vice versa.

This decision was a crucial one for Eckhart as a metaphysician and theologian. He was dissociating himself from the Thomistic notion of being and proposing a new metaphysics based on the principle that "understanding is superior to existence and belongs to a different order."[20]

This would seem to put Eckhart on the side of common sense, for it is certainly reasonable to think that an intellectual being is superior in perfection to a mere being, like a stone. How can being be elevated above knowing and considered to be the proper name of God? This is so sensible that some 'transcendental Thomists' today are persuaded, like Eckhart, that in God intelligence is more fundamental and primary than being.[21]

19 See Duns Scotus, *Reportata Parisiensia*, I, d. 8, q. 1; vol. XI, p. 71.

20 Below, p. 46.

21 See B. Lonergan, *Insight. A Study of Human Understanding* (London, New York, 1957), p. 677: "Among Thomists, however, there is a dispute whether *ipsum intelligere* or

And yet, as Eckhart well knew, St. Thomas defended the primacy and superiority of being (*esse*) over knowing (*intelligere*), at least when they are considered in themselves and in their own natures. Being in itself is more perfect than living, and living is more perfect than knowing. Aquinas justifies this paradoxical position on the ground that being, taken in itself, includes every perfection of being: life and understanding are not perfections added to being from outside; they are modes of being included in being itself. Being, living, and knowing can be considered in still another way according to Aquinas — as they are participated in by a subject. Then, Aquinas teaches, knowing is more perfect than living, and living is more perfect than being. For when being is participated in by a subject it is not present in its total perfection. The being of any creature is limited and finite, determined to the nature or essence of the creature. Thus a stone participates in being more imperfectly than a living being, and a living being more imperfectly than an intellectual being. In this perspective, then, an intellectual being is more excellent than something that is merely a being. Being (*esse*), however, taken just in itself is prior in excellence to all other perfections and it includes them within itself. This is why, according to Aquinas, *ipsum esse,* being itself, is the most fitting name of God.[22]

Eckhart leaves us in no doubt about his attitude toward this Thomistic position. After explaining it he frankly says: "I

ipsum esse subsistens is logically first among divine attributes. As has been seen in the section on the notion of God, all other divine attributes follow from the notion of an unrestricted act of understanding. Moreover, since we define being by its relation to intelligence, necessarily our ultimate is not being but intelligence." See John of St. Thomas, *Cursus Theologicus* (Paris, 1934) II, p. 339, n. 11: "... ergo ipsum intelligere, ut est actus ultimus et formaliter constituit vitam intellectivam ut non determinabilem ab alio, formaliter constituit eam in ratione summi gradus et naturae divinae."

22 St. Thomas, *Summa Theol.* I, 4, 2, ad 3; I-II, 2, 5, ad 2; *In Divinis Nominibus*, c. 5, lect. 1; ed. C. Pera (Rome, 1950), pp. 235-236, n. 632-635.

believe the exact opposite to be true."[23] For him, knowing is more excellent than being and it belongs to a higher order. So the name 'Intellect' is more appropriate to God than being or existence. Indeed, Eckhart in the Parisian Questions goes so far as to deny that God can properly be called a being or existent. A being is strictly speaking a creature of the intelligence that is God. We can call God a being, but we are then transferring a term to him by analogy, as we may call diet 'healthy' because it is related to the health that formally exists only in a living being. Being is not God, but the creation of God, and if we call God being it is because of this relation to his creature.

As Eckhart uses the term 'being' or 'existence' in these Parisian Questions it essentially includes a relation to a cause. Citing the Neoplatonic *Book of Causes,* he says that existence is the first of creatures. This notion of being was not unknown to previous scholastics.[24] St. Albert derives 'existence' from the Latin words 'ex' and 'sistere', which mean 'to stand out'. In this interpretation, to say that something exists means that it stands outside of its cause.[25] Henry of Ghent explicates the meaning of existence in much the same way: for him, the existence of a creature is its relation to God as its efficient cause. Eckhart's anonymous citation of Henry of Ghent and his quotation of the *Book of Causes* on the meaning of existence are convincing proof that his own notion of existence falls in the same Neoplatonic tradition.[26]

23 See below, p. 47.

24 See below, p. 46.

25 St. Albert, *In I Sent.* q. 5, a. 6; ed. Borgnet (Paris, 1893), vol. 25, p. 184. See Richard of St. Victor, *De Trinitate*, IV, 12; PL 196, 937D-938D.

26 See below, pp. 45-46. St. Thomas, writing in a Neoplatonic context, refers to this notion of existence: "[Dionysius] ostendit quod ens dictum de Deo, signat processum existentium a Deo." *In Divinis Nominibus*, p. 235, n. 632.

Against this background it is clearly improper to say that God 'exists', for he has no cause. The proper use of language requires us to say that he is not a being or existent, but the cause of being and existence. God is properly an intellect, and indeed pure intelligence. This is Eckhart's position in the Parisian Questions and it is also his in his commentaries on Scripture. There we read that "Intellect is the nature of God, and his being is understanding." Again, God is "pure understanding ... in his essence he is totally an intellect."[27]

One of Eckhart's statements condemned by his accusers is: "There is something in the soul that is uncreated und uncreatable; if the whole soul were of this nature it would be uncreated and uncreatable; and this is the intellect."[28] In his reply to his critics Eckhart explained that he was talking about a pure intellect such as God, not about the human intellect, which is a created faculty of the soul. The human soul is not pure intellect: it is only 'intellectual', that is, it participates in intellectuality, having been created in the image and likeness of God.[29]

In this perspective, then, being or existence is foreign to intelligence. The intellect and all of the instruments it uses, such as ideas and cognitive likenesses, and everything associated with it, such as truth, and mathematics, do not have the nature of being. If ideas or cognitive likenesses, by which we know things, were beings, they would prevent our knowing them; they would themselves be objects known and they would not be vehicles whereby we know other things. In order to perform their instrumental function they must be void of being.

27 *Expositio libri Genesi; LW*, vol. 1, p. 52; see *Expositio sancti evangelii secundum Johannem; LW*, vol. 3, p. 27, n. 34, p. 32, n. 38.

28 G. Théry, *art. cit.*, p. 214, n. 8; J. M. Clark, *Meister Eckhart. An Introduction to the Study of his Works* (London, etc. 1957), pp. 256-257.

29 G. Théry, *art. cit.*, p. 201, n. 6; R. B. Blakney, *op. cit.*, p. 269, n. 6.

Eckhart finds confirmation of his thesis that an intellect as such is not a being in Aristotle's description of intellect. According to the Stagirite, the intellect must be devoid of everything it understands; as Anaxagoras, says, "it must be pure from all admixture," so that it can know all things.[30] Suppose sight had a particular color; we would then see only that one color and not all colors. So too, if the intellect had a particular nature of its own it could not know all natures. This shows that it has nothing in common with anything it knows. To St. Thomas Aquinas this is convincing proof that the intellect has no particular sensible nature and hence that it is immaterial.[31] For his part, Eckhart draws a more radical conclusion, that the intellect as such has no being at all, in short that it is nothing (*nihil*).[32]

Eckhart, the theologian, also finds in Scripture grounds for saying that God is an intellect and not a being or an existent. John did not say "In the beginning was Being, and God was Being," but "In the beginning was the Word, and the Word was with God, and the Word was God."[33] Christ did not say "I am Being," but "I am the Truth."[34] Eckhart points out that the terms 'word' and 'truth' are meaningful only in relation to intelligence.

Some scriptural exegetes believe that God revealed his name as 'Being' when he replied to Moses' request for his name "I am who am." St. Augustine and other Fathers of the Church, followed by St. Thomas Aquinas, interpreted the text of Exodus 3:14 in this way.[35] Eckhart, anticipating a modern exegesis of

30 Aristotle, *De Anima*, III, 4, 429a 19; 429b 22-24.

31 St. Thomas, *In III De Anima*, lect. 7; ed. Pirotta (Rome, 1936), n. 680-681.

32 See below, p. 51.

33 John 1, 1.

34 John 14, 6.

35 See St. Augustine, *De Trinitate*, V, 2, 3; CCL 50 (Turnholt, 1968), pp. 207-208. See also E. Gilson, *History of Christian Philosophy in the Middle Ages* (New York, 1955),

this passage, sees it rather as a concealment of the divine name.[36] If a man accosted at night is asked his name and he wishes to conceal his identity, he will reply "I am who I am." In Eckhart's view this was also God's intent when he made his reply to Moses.[37]

At the end of Question 1 Eckhart allays his reader's fears that his denial of being or existence to God derogates from his perfection. On the contrary, Eckhart assures us, this negative approach to God is the best of all. We must deny of him all created perfections, in their proper and formal meaning, in order to come as close to him as we can. Existence is not present in God but rather "purity of existence." In the context Eckhart means that God is pure *from* existence: he is void of existence in the creaturely sense of the term.[38] But, as we shall presently see,[39] negative statements about God, in Eckhart's view, amount to the best affirmation we can make about him. He denies existence and other creaturely perfections of God only to affirm most vehemently that, as the ground and cause of all things, he precontains all of them in an ideal and perfect state. In this sense, God has the purity and fullness of being: being unmixed with non-being and finiteness, such as it is present in creatures.

pp. 70-72. For St. Thomas' doctrine, see *Summa Theol.* I, 13, 11; E. Gilson, *op. cit.*, pp. 368-369.

36 See below, p. 48. For a similar modern exegesis of this text, see A. M. Dubarle, "La signification du nom de Yahweh," *Revue des sciences philosophiques et théologiques*, 35 (1951), pp. 5-21; M. M. Bourke, "Yahweh, the Divine Name," *The Bridge*, 3 (1958), pp. 272-287; C. de Vogel, "'Ego sum qui sum' et sa signification pour une philosophie chrétienne," *Revue des sciences religieuses*, 35 (1961), 337-355.

37 See below, p. 48.

38 See E. Gilson, *op. cit.*, pp. 438-439: "In these Questions, then, Eckhart considers God as One who has the privilege of being pure of all being." See also E. Gilson, *Being and Some Philosophers*, 2nd ed. (Toronto, 1952), p. 39. On the meaning of *puritas essendi* see V. Lossky, *Théologie négative et connaissance de Dieu chez Maître Eckhart* (Paris, 1960), pp. 134-135.

39 See below, p. 33.

And this too, Eckhart concludes, is contained in the meaning of God's reply to Moses: "I am who am."

This alerts us to the paradox at the heart of Eckhart's conception of God: he does not 'exist' and yet he supremely exists; he is 'nothing' and yet he is all things. Surely more light needs to be shed on this seeming contradiction; but this will have to wait until we come to the Prologues to the *Opus Tripartitum*.

The second Parisian Question asks whether an angel's knowing is identical with his existence. Eckhart specifies that he is talking about an angel's knowing (*intelligere*) as an act exercized by him. This is to avoid a misunderstanding, for Aquinas speaks of *intelligere* not only as an act but also as the very being (*esse*) of an intellectual creature.[40]

As in the previous Question Eckhart politely gives the first word to Thomas Aquinas, who argued in his *Summa* that an angelic act of knowing cannot be the same as his act of existing, because the former is unlimited and extends to everything whereas the latter is determined to the angel's particular nature.[41] Eckhart accepts the validity of this reasoning, but he hastens to add his own proofs, all of which depend on his own notion of being. As he uses the term here and in the previous Question, a being or existent properly speaking is a definite, determinate something, located in a genus and species. Now, as we have seen, an intellect as such is not a being but is open to all being. It is not located in time or place but is atemporal and aspatial. Of course, only God's intellect has these characteristics

40 "Intelligere autem quandoque sumitur pro operatione; et sic principium ejus est potentia vel habitus; quandoque vero pro ipso esse intellectualis naturae; et sic principium ejus quod est intelligere est ipsa essentia animae intellectivae." *De Spiritualibus Creaturis*, XI, ad 14. See *Summa Theol.* I, 18, 2, ad 1.; also J. Robb, "Intelligere intelligentibus est esse," *An Etienne Gilson Tribute*, ed. C. J. O'Neil (Milwaukee, 1959), pp. 209-227.

41 St. Thomas, *Summa Theol.* I, 54, 2.

in their purity, for he alone is a pure intellect. An angelic intellect is not a pure intellect: it is a natural power of the angel, and this identifies it as *something*; but insofar as it is an intellect it is indeterminate and no-thing. It tends to be no-thing, not because it is above being, like the divine intellect, but because it is below being. God is superior to being as its cause; a created intellect is below being because it is caused and determined by an object outside itself, and this object is a being. Thus the created intellect of an angel shares in the indetermination proper to every intellect, and it cannot be identified with the angelic existence, which is something definite and determined in a genus and species.

The third Question is a disputation held in Paris by the Franciscan Gonsalvo of Spain and the Dominican Eckhart. Gonsalvo argues for the essential superiority of the will over the intellect; Eckhart, following St. Thomas, takes the opposite stand. The Franciscans and Dominicans generally differ on the importance they give to these two faculties, the Franciscans giving preference to the will and the Dominicans to the intellect.[42]

Gonsalvo believed that human happiness consists essentially in the love of God, not in knowledge of him. Indeed, he held that it is more excellent to love God in this life than to know him in heaven. Eckhart supports the essential superiority of intellect over will: a stand that is hardly surprising in view of his identification of God with pure intellect. In us, intellect is our highest faculty because it enables us to reach God in his hidden depths and not under the veil of goodness or being.

42 St. Bonaventure expresses this difference well when he says that Dominicans give themselves first to speculation and study and second to devotion (*unctio*), while Franciscans give themselves first to devotion and second to speculation. *In Hexameron*, coll. 22, 25; *Opera Omnia* V (Quaracchi, 1891), p. 440.

In a German sermon Eckhart refers to this school debate:

> I once said in the school [of Paris] that intellect was nobler than will; and yet both belong to this light [i.e. the higher light of revealed truth]. Then a master in another school [Gonsalvo] said that the will was nobler than the intellect, for the will takes things as they are in themselves, while the intellect takes the things as they are in her. That is true. An eye is nobler in itself than an eye painted on the wall. I say again, however, that intellect is nobler than will. The will apprehends God under the garment of goodness. The intellect apprehends God naked, as He is, divested of goodness and being. Goodness is a garment under which God is hidden.[43]

Eckhart is here defending the superiority of the intellect on the grounds that it knows God purely, not covered by creaturely garments of goodness or being. Gonsalvo contends that the will is nobler than the intellect because it goes out to things as they are in themselves, whereas the intellect takes things into itself and knows them as they exist in it. So it is better to love God than to know him, even in heaven. This distinction between the ways the intellect and will relate to their objects was taught by St. Thomas; and on its basis he concluded that *in this life* it is better to love God than to know him.[44] But he denied that the will in itself is superior to the intellect or that it is better to love God than to know him in heaven. Eckhart defends the nobility of the intellect on the unthomistic ground that it penetrates to God beyond both goodness and being.

In this Question, as in the first, Eckhart considers God to be pure intelligence, uncreatable, subsistent, and void of being. We

43 J. M. Clark, *Meister Eckhart. An Introduction to the Study of his Works*, pp. 208-209.

44 St. Thomas, *Summa Theol.* I, 82, 3.

are made in the image of God precisely because we have a faculty of knowing. Ours is not a pure intellect like God's, but we share in intelligence, and it is because of this that we resemble him and can be united to him. Eckhart often speaks the language of a mystic when he describes the element in the soul whereby it encounters God. It is the highest and most intimate part of the soul, the ground of the soul (*Grund der Seele*) or spark of the soul (*scintilla animae, Seelenfünklein*).[45]

This deep and hidden part of the soul is the point where the Word of God is born within us; here we achieve true contemplation and become one with God, united to him by both vision and love. Eckhart identifies this point of the soul as the power of intellect, though he sometimes locates it beyond all the powers of the soul. In this Question it is the intellect that is said to bring us closest to God, to conform us with him, and to 'deify' us. It is also said to be the ground of our freedom and the seat of sanctifying grace, which makes us pleasing to God. We could hardly imagine a greater apotheosis of the intellect and the intellectual life.

The fourth Question raises a problem in the philosophy of nature: Can there be motion without a terminus or end? This is an unusual topic for Eckhart. To judge from his literary remains, he seems to have almost completely ignored this branch of philosophy.

The problem and its solution originate in Aristotle's *Physics*.[46] Aristotle raises the question whether it is possible for

45 See J. Ancelet-Hustache, *Master Eckhart and the Rhineland Mystics* (New York, London, 1957), pp. 65-66. For the notion of "spark of the soul" see Hans Hof, *Scintilla Animae* (Lund, Bonn, 1952); K. G. Kertz, "Meister Eckhart's Teaching on the Birth of the Divine Word in the Soul," *Traditio*, 15 (1959), 327-363.

46 Aristotle, *Physics*, VI, 6, 236b 33.

there to be continuous motion or change without something having been changed or moved, or is motion or change always from something to something. His reply is that all change or motion implies a starting point and terminal point. This is true even in movement that appeared 'endless' to the ancient astronomers: the motion of the heavens. This motion takes place over a period of time, and since time is divisible a prior part of the motion must have been completed before a subsequent part. On this ground Aristotle argues that any present motion must have been preceded by a prior motion, so that "everything that is moved must have been moved before."[47]

Eckhart accepts Aristotle's reasoning and concludes that all motion implies a terminus or end. Turning to the question of the most important motion for the medieval physicist, the motion of the heavens, he distinguishes between three meanings of the word terminus or end: the starting point of the motion (*terminus a quo*), the subject of the motion (*terminus in quo*), and the purpose of the motion (here called the *terminus ad quem*). Ignoring the first meaning of terminus, he identifies the subject of motion as the 'first mobile body' or the outermost heavenly sphere, whose circular movement, according to ancient and medieval astronomy, causes all other motion and change in the universe.[48] As for the purpose of its motion, Eckhart, like St. Thomas, was not satisfied with the teaching of the ancients, that the heavens move simply in order to cause generation and corruption in the sublunar world.[49] In the Christian scheme of things its purpose

47 "Motus enim ex ipsa sui ratione repugnat ne possit poni finis, eo quod motus est in aliud tendens; unde non habet rationem finis, sed magis ejus quod est ad finem." St. Thomas, *De Potentia*, V, 5.

48 See St. Thomas, *In XII Metaph*. lect. 9, n. 2558 ff.

49 See St. Thomas, *De Potentia*, V, 5.

must be nobler than this. Universal Nature, of which it is the highest embodiment, is like a father who looks after the welfare of his whole family. Thus the heavens, and especially the first heavenly sphere, dominates and controls the whole natural order, and its movement is intended to serve the well being of the whole universe.

The fifth and final Question takes up another problem in medieval physics as it relates to the interpretation of the death of Christ.

According to medieval physics there are four elements: fire, air, water, and earth, which combine in various mixtures to form 'mixed bodies', for example the human body. The scholastics debated at length the manner in which elements are present in a 'mixed body'. St. Thomas wrote a brief treatise "On the Mixture of the Elements" in which he opposes Avicenna's solution of this problem.[50] The Arabian philosopher held that the elements remain in a 'mixed body' with their own substantial forms; St. Thomas on the contrary argues that the forms of the elements are not actually but only virtually present in a 'mixed body'.

Eckhart agrees with his Dominican confrère that a 'mixed body' can have actually but one substantial form. His reason is that a substantial form gives a body its substantial existence: if the elements remained in the composite with their own forms, it would not be one substance but an accidental grouping of four bodies. The human body, then, would not be one substantial entity but a mixture of four substances. What is at stake is the substantial unity of a living body. According to both Aquinas and

50 St. Thomas, *De Mixtione Elementorum*, ed. J. Perrier, *Opuscula Omnia* (Paris, 1949), pp. 19-22. For Avicenna's doctrine, see *Sufficientia*, I, c. 10 (Venice, 1508), fol. 19. Averroes criticized Avicenna's views on this matter; see his *In III De Caelo et Mundo*, c. 67 (Venice, 1574), V, pp. 226-227.

Eckhart this unity would be compromised if there were actually more than one substantial form in the body.[51]

The question of the unity of substantial form was hotly disputed at the time.[52] St. Thomas' opinion was condemned by Robert Kilwardby, archbishop of Canterbury, and by his successor John Pecham because of the theological implications they saw in it.[53] One of their main objections was that if there were only one substantial form in Christ's body (his intellectual soul), at death his body could no longer be called his. At the separation of body from soul, the body would no longer be identical with Christ's body. In order to obviate this difficulty they posited a substantial 'form of corporeity' in man, distinct from his intellectual soul, which remained the same in Christ's body before and after death. Aquinas for his part saw no need for such a special substantial form. While maintaining that Christ really died on the cross, with the resultant separation of soul and body, he insisted that Christ's body remained identical before and after death owing to its hypostatic union with the divine Person.[54]

This appears to be the solution of this theological problem adopted by Eckhart. His account of the process of dying follows closely that of St. Thomas. When a living body dies, a process of corruption begins in which its substantial form, or soul, ceases to inform the body, and intermediate forms take its place until the body disintegrates into its original four elements. At this point the elements recover their own substantial forms. The

51 Among other texts of St. Thomas, see *De Spiritualibus Creaturis*, 3; ed. L. W. Keeler (Rome, 1938); *Summa Theol.* I, 76, 3-4.

52 See E. Gilson, *History of Christian Philosophy in the Middle Ages*, pp. 416-420. For the beginnings of this debate, see D. A. Callus, "The Origins of the Problem of the Unity of Form," *The Thomist*, 24 (1961), pp. 257-285.

53 See E. Gilson, *ibid.*, pp. 417-418.

54 See St. Thomas, *Quodl.* II, 1; III, 4; XII, 9; *Summa Theol.* III, 50, 4-5.

intermediate forms that mediate the process of corruption are not the perfect forms of the elements of the 'mixed body'; they are in fact so imperfect that they do not place the body in a genus or species.[55] For example, the form of a dead body ('corpse') does not locate the body in a positive genus or species, as does the substantial form, or soul, of the living body. Rather, it is an accidental form that does not give a positive being to a body but only a privation. These imperfect and transient forms, and the qualities attendant upon them (such as the pallid color of a corpse), do not really name the corrupting body except in a privative way.

Christ's death was similar to that of any man's. In the process of dying his soul ceased to inform his body and intermediate forms took its place. Eckhart did not believe, as did Richard Knapwell, that these intermediate forms gave to Christ's body a new species and nature.[56] Nor did he believe that they were united hypostatically to the divine person of Christ. In the process of dying, everything happened to Christ as to other men: the difference lay in the fact that throughout his dying and at his death his complete human nature, soul and body, remained united to his divine Person.

2. *The Prologues.*

After the denial of being or existence to God in the Parisian Questions it comes as a surprise to find Eckhart identifying

55 St. Thomas, *In I De Generatione et Corruptione*, lect. 8, n. 3 (Rome, 1886), 3, p. 292.

56 Knapwell was a Dominican master in theology who opposed Pecham's condemnation of the Thomistic doctrine in 1286. In that year Pecham, the archbishop of Canterbury, condemned as heretical the doctrine of Knapwell: "... in morte (Christi) fuit introducta nova forma substantialis, et nova species, vel natura, quamvis non nova assumptione vel unione Verbo copulata." See Peckham, *Registrum Epistolarum Fr. Johannes Peckham*, ed. C. T. Martin (London, 1885), vol. 3, p. 922.

existence with God in the Prologues to the *Opus Tripartitum*. In the Questions creatures are said to exist in the proper sense of the term, while God is above existence as its cause; in the Prologues God is said to exist whereas creatures are nothing in themselves. Did Eckhart change his mind between these works or is this contradiction reconcilable? Some historians believe that these works represent two different phases in Eckhart's doctrinal development; but this is difficult to support in the absence of more firm dating of some of his works. The more general opinion is that the contradiction is more verbal than real: Eckhart did not radically change his doctrine but adopted a different perspective in the two writings while his thought remained consistent.[57] This is a problem we shall have to return to at the end of our analysis.

Both in the General Prologue and the Prologue to the *Book of Propositions* Eckhart defends at length the fundamental thesis of the *Opus Tripartitum*: "Existence is God (*Esse est Deus*)." He begins with an elucidation of terms. 'Being' (*ens*) means nothing but 'existence' (*esse*), just as 'one' means nothing but 'oneness', 'true' nothing but 'truth', and 'good' nothing but 'goodness'. In short, *ens* for Eckhart, as for St. Thomas, is a concrete term whose whole meaning is conveyed by the abstract word *esse*.[58] Hence we shall not betray the mind of Eckhart if we translate *ens* by 'being' or 'a being' and *esse* by the abstract 'beingness' or 'existence'. In his German sermons he himself uses the word 'istikeit' ('is-ness') as an equivalent for *esse*.[59]

57 See V. Lossky, *op. cit.*, pp. 210-220; E. Gilson, *History of Christian Philosophy in the Middle Ages*, p. 439; F. Copleston, *A History of Philosophy* vol. 3, part 1 (New York, 1963), p. 198.

58 See below, p. 78. See St. Thomas, *In Boethium de Hebdomadibus*, 2; ed. Mandonnet, *Opuscula* (Paris, 1927), I, p. 171.

59 Other forms of the word are 'istikeide', 'istekeit'. See Fr. Pfeiffer, *Meister Eckhart* (Göttingen, 1914), p. 37, line 35, p. 204, line 21, p. 310, line 40. For the English trans-

Eckhart's model for this analysis of the word 'being' is taken from Aristotle. The Stagirite says that the word 'white' (*album*) indicates nothing but the quality of whiteness (*albedinem*).[60] In this respect it is unlike a generic or specific word like 'animal' or 'man', which signifies a substance as qualitatively differentiated. These words signify some thing as possessing a distinctive nature or essence. According to Eckhart, 'being' is not a generic or specific word, nor does it signify like one: its whole meaning is contained in its abstract equivalent 'existence' or 'is-ness'. No generic or specific subject accompanies it, for if it did it would have to be other than being; but in fact what is other than being is nothing. St. Thomas, before Eckhart, offered a similar explanation of the meaning of being: "Being (*ens*)", he wrote, "does not signify a quiddity but only the act of existing."[61] The question remains whether Eckhart conceives being or existence in the same way as St. Thomas. We shall see that he does not.

Eckhart finds reasons for identifying existence with God both in Scripture and among the philosophers. In the Book of Exodus God revealed his name as 'I am who am' or 'He who is': a clear proof that he alone properly speaking is being or existence.[62] Philosophers have also reached the notion of God as absolute existence, especially the "first philosophers" Parmenides and Melissus, who taught that there is but one being. Eckhart had no first hand knowledge of the writings of these Eleatics, but through the accounts of their philosophy in the writings of

lation of these sermons, see R. B. Blakney, *Meister Eckhart. A Modern Translation* (New York, London, 1941), pp. 160, 180, 204.

60 Aristotle, *Categories*, c. 5, 3b 19-20.

61 "Ens autem non dicit quidditatem, sed solum actum essendi, cum sit principium ipsum." St. Thomas, *In I Sent.*, d. 8, q. 4, a. 2, ad 2; ed. Mandonnet (Paris, 1929), I, p. 223.

62 Exodus 3: 14. See below, p. 94.

Aristotle and Avicenna he grasped the profound significance of their analysis of being, and he basically agreed with them that being is in essence one, incapable of non-being, eternal, unchanging, admitting of no difference or otherness. In this he was not the first in the Middle Ages: St. Bonaventure gives a similar analysis of being when treating of the divine names in his *Journey of the Mind to God.*[63]

Eckhart offers five arguments to show that existence is God, all of which strike the same note: God is simply not God as traditionally known unless he is identical with existence. If existence were something different from him, he would owe his existence to it, and he would not be the first or uncreated being. This other entity would be his God, and he would not be God. Of course Eckhart presupposes that existence is not just a word, as some modern positivists believe, but a reality.[64] It is that reality by which all things exist, as whiteness is a real quality by which all white things are white.

Eckhart's identification of existence with God renders almost superfluous a proof of his existence. It is hardly conceivable for Eckhart that existence should not exist! The statement "Existence is God" is like the tautology "Man is man." Since there is no truer statement than one in which the same thing is predicated of itself, it is certainly true that God exists.

This enables us to measure the distance between Eckhart and Aquinas. Faced with the same argument for the self-evidence of God's existence, Aquinas granted its validity only for one who enjoyed the vision of God in heaven; here below we do not see the essence of God or the identity of his essence with his

63 St. Bonaventure, *Itinerarium Mentis in Deum*, 5; *Opera Omnia* V (Quaracchi, 1891), pp. 308-310.

64 See Sidney Hook, *The Quest for Being* (New York, 1961), p. 147.

existence, so we have to demonstrate his existence from his effects.[65] Eckhart's approach to God is not in the Thomistic but the Anselmian tradition, for he finds the evidence of God's existence immediately available in our notion of him.[66]

Not only does Eckhart identify God with existence but also with unity, truth, and goodness. This follows from the fact that being and its transcendental properties are convertible: it is equally true to say "Being is one" and "One is being." Hence the transcendentals are identical with being; and since God is pure being he is also pure unity, truth, and goodness. Their identity in God, however, does not exclude a relationship between them: according to Eckhart goodness and truth are grounded in being, and being itself is established in unity.[67] Unity, then, is more primary and fundamental in God than being or any of the other transcendentals. This places Eckhart squarely in the Neoplatonic tradition, which makes the One the first principle of all things and being the first of its emanations.[68] His citations from Boethius, Proclus, and the author of the *Book of Causes* on the unity of the first principle or God is clear proof of the source of his doctrine.[69]

God, then, is, above all, One or pure Unity; but Eckhart has still to tell us what this means. Unity is a negative notion,

65 See St. Thomas, *Contra Gentiles*, I, 10, n. 4; 11, n. 5. Notice that St. Thomas uses the same example of a tautology: Man is man. See also, *Summa Theol.*, I, 2, 1, obj. 2 and ad 2.

66 See St. Anselm, *Proslogion*, ed. F. S. Schmitt, *Sancti Anselmi Opera Omnia* (Seckau, 1933), I, pp. 97, 122; transl. by M. J. Charlesworth, *St. Anselm's Proslogion* (Oxford, 1965). See also A. C. Pegis, "St. Anselm and the Argument of the 'Proslogion'," *Mediaeval Studies* 28 (1966), 228-267.

67 See below, p. 96.

68 See Plotinus, *Enneads*, V, 1, 5, lines 3-7; V, 5, 10, lines 11-14. For him, however, being can only participate in unity, it cannot be identical with it. VI, 9, 2, lines 17-24.

69 See below, pp. 95-96.

meaning an absence of division, or indivision. What is one is not divided. But how can a negation apply to God? Negation places a limitation on a being. If we say that one thing is not another we assert a limitation on that thing: it is restricted to being itself and it is *not* something else. At the same time we assert a multiplicity, for a negation implies a plurality. But God is pure being, knowing no limitation, restriction or plurality. Hence terms implying a negation, like 'other', 'different', or 'multiple' do not apply to him. We must deny negation of him, so that the negation proper to him is the 'negation of negation'. By the 'negation of negation' we conceive of God most purely as One or Unity. Paradoxically the 'negation of negation' is at the same time the purest and strongest affirmation we can make of God, for the double negation amounts to an affirmation. In a sermon Eckhart says,

> The negation of negation is the quintessence, purity, and doubling of affirmed being. Exodus 3 [14]: "I am who am." Hence it is aptly said: "Show us the Father" (that is, the One) "and it is enough for us."[70]

Eckhart here interprets the divine being in terms of unity. He sees in the revealed name "I am who am", with its repetition of 'am', the purest affirmation, and the exclusion of every negation, that befit God alone. Its meaning is the same as the 'negation of negation'.[71] The vision of the Father in heaven, who revealed his name as 'being' is the vision of him as One.

Having identified existence with God, Eckhart is faced with the difficult problem of accounting for the existence of creatures.

70 See text in V. Lossky, *Théologie négative et connaissance de Dieu chez Maitre Eckhart* (Paris, 1960), p. 68, n. 103.

71 *Ibid.*

How can there be anything besides God if he is existence itself? Eckhart denies that there can be anything outside of, or besides, being or existence. Creatures exist within existence, that is to say within God and through the divine existence.[72] Eckhart's justification of this bold stand engages him in some of his most abstruse metaphysical speculation.

Creatures differ from God in that he is existence pure and simple whereas they are this or that being, this or that sort of being. Similarly God is absolute unity, truth, and goodness, while a creature is this or that one, true, or good thing. The qualification of *this* or *that* adds nothing positive to being or the transcendentals; it simply indicates a limitation on them. Hence the being, unity, truth, and goodness of creatures add nothing to those of God. Indeed, apart from God, or outside of him, creatures are absolutely nothing.[73] This is the meaning of the statement Eckhart often repeated in his sermons and which was condemned by Pope John XXII:

> All creatures are a mere nothing. I do not say that they are something trifling, or even that they are something, but that they are a mere nothing, for no creature has existence.[74]

Eckhart's critics saw in this an outright denial of the existence of creatures, but this was not his intention; on the contrary he protested that he was firmly grounding their existence in God.[75]

72 See below, p. 89.

73 *Ibid.*

74 See G. Théry "Edition critique des pièces relatives au procès d'Eckhart contenues dans le manuscrit 33b de la bibliothèque de Soest," p. 184, n. 15. In his reply Eckhart defends the proposition as a "devout and useful truth, leading to the formation of character, contempt of the world, love of God, and love of him alone." See *ibid.*, p. 205, n. 15; transl. Blakney, *op. cit.*, p. 272, n. 15. In his German treatises Eckhart emphasizes that the soul must lose itself, and even God: "The soul must subsist in absolute nothingness." F. Pfeiffer, *Meister Eckhart*, transl. by C. de B. Evans, p. 274.

75 See below, p. 100.

His teaching on this point always remained the same: God, as existence itself, is immediately present to creatures, and they exist through him and in him alone. But this does not imply that they possess an existence of their own, different from that of God; for God is existence.[76]

Eckhart elucidates this through the analogy of the relation of the soul to the body, an analogy based on the Neoplatonic notion that God is in the world as the soul is in the body.[77] Now the soul gives the body existence and life by directly informing it. The soul is intimately present to the whole body and to every part of it without being divided or changed or corrupted by them. In itself it transcends the body and is outside of it, and yet it penetrates the body and makes it share in its existence and life. Similarly God, as existence itself, is entirely present to every creature, directly giving it existence, while he himself transcends his creation and suffers no division or change. He is the one being, life, and actuality of all things, but in himself he remains aloof from them.

Eckhart uses a Thomistic notion to express the intimate relationship of God to creatures, hile giving it a new interpretation. St. Thomas describes being (*esse*) as the perfection or actuality of all things, even of forms.[78] The being so described

76 Eckhart sometimes says that a creature possesses (*habet*) existence, unity, etc., while emphasizing that existence and unity are God. See below, p. 98. E. Gilson interprets Eckhart's thought in this way: "Being is, so to speak, imputed to beings by God without ever becoming their own being, about in the same way as, in Luther's theology, justice will be imputed to the just without ever becoming their own justice." *History of Christian Philosophy in the Middle Ages*, p. 441. J. Koch disagreed: he believed that according to Eckhart God not only imputes being and the transcendentals to creatures, but truly gives them "a flowing, fleeting being." J. Koch, "Zur Analogielehre Meister Eckharts," *Mélanges offerts à E. Gilson* (Toronto, Paris, 1959), p. 342. But this creaturely being is not a distinct act of existing possessed by creatures as their own, as St. Thomas teaches; it can be nothing but the divine existence as formally participated by creatures.

77 See below, pp. 98-99. See B. Muller-Thym, *The Establishment of the University of Being in the Doctrine of Meister Eckhart of Hochheim* (New York, 1939), pp. 14-27.

78 St. Thomas, *Summa Theol.* I, 4, 1, ad 3.

is the created act of existing (*actus essendi*) which, in his view, actualizes the essence or form of a creature and thus posits it in existence.

Eckhart quotes this description of *esse* and adopts it as his own; but the *esse* he has in mind is not a created existence. It is the divine existence as it diffuses itself in creatures and establishes them in existence.[79] The notion of a created act of existing in the Thomistic sense appears to be totally lacking in Eckhart's metaphysics. As we have seen, he interprets *esse* as God, and it is by this *esse* alone that all creatures exist. There is no intermediary created existence by which they exist, no created unity, truth or goodness by which they are one, true or good.

Though he may on occasion use Thomistic language, Eckhart's own metaphysical notions are usually far removed from those of St. Thomas. In particular, the Thomistic notion of *esse* as the act of existing is foreign to his mind. In his Latin works he likens *esse* to an essential form (*forma essentialis*)[80] in which creatures participate in order to exist, on the analogy of the soul whose life and existence are shared by the body.

In defending his proposition that "Existence is God" Eckhart at first sight appears to make room for a created existence different from the existence of God. He explained to his accusers

79 See G. Théry, *op. cit.*, p. 193, n. 3; transl. by Blakney, *op. cit.*, p. 264, n. 3. *Esse* is the "actualitas formalis omnis formae universaliter et essentiae;" *LW* I, p. 175. See V. Lossky, *op. cit.*, p. 156: "Les expressions que Maître Eckhart emprunte à saint Thomas pour parler de l'*esse* comme d'une actualité universelle ne désignent pas l'acte d'exister conféré à une essence par l'efficace divine, un acte fini par lequel l'essence existe, mais l'action même de Dieu, la présence active de la Cause première dans le fond secret des êtres créés." God, as wisdom, is also identified as the actuality of all forms: "Deus autem sapientia ipse est actualitas et forma actuum omnium et formarum." *Expos. in Sap.*, ed. G. Théry, *op. cit.*, IV, p. 287, n. 4-5.

80 See *LW*, I, p. 174. According to Eckhart every substantial form is *esse* and gives *esse*. See *In Exodum*, I, *LW*, II, p. 55, line 11; *In Iohannem, LW*, III, p. 287, lines 3-4. This derives from Boethius, *De Trinitate*, c. 2; PL 64, 1250 B.

that the proposition is true if understood of ***absolute*** existence, but not of *formally inherent* existence.[81] But this is not meant to be a distinction between two different existences, one divine and uncreated, the other created. Absolute existence is God as he is in himself, transcending creatures; formally inherent existence is the same existence as it is immanent in creatures, penetrating and touching them, so to speak, in order to make them exist.

It has been shown that Eckhart is here following the model of St. Albert's conception of the soul and its relation to the body.[82] St. Albert distinguished between two ways in which the soul can be regarded: in itself and in its role as the form and perfection of the body. In itself the soul is an absolute and simple substance, but as a form it diffuses itself in the body and gives it existence and life. The body has no existence or life of its own but only that which it has within the soul. In an analogous manner Eckhart conceives of existence as an absolute reality in itself; in short, as God; but through creation this existence diffuses itself in the universe, giving it existence within itself. In its absolute character, then, the divine existence is the only reality; outside of it there is nothing.

This description of God as existence undoubtedly contradicts the *Parisian Questions*. There, being and existence are denied of God and he is declared to be pure intellect, which is superior to being. It should be noticed, however, that in the *Parisian Questions* Eckhart uses the term *esse* to mean a definite, limited thing, in other words an effect of God or a creature.[83] In this

81 G. Théry, *op. cit.*, I, p. 193, n. 5; Blakney, *op. cit.*, p. 264, n. 5.

82 See B. Muller-Thym, *The Establishment of the University of Being in the Doctrine of Meister Eckhart of Hochheim* (New York, 1939), p. 88. For St. Albert's doctrine of the soul, see E. Gilson, "L'Ame raisonnable chez Albert le Grand," *Archives d'histoire doctrinale et littéraire du moyen âge*, 14 (1943-44), 5-72.

83 See below, p. 46.

sense of the term he also denies being of God in the *Opus Tripartitum*: God is not *this* or *that* being, but being pure and simple. Again, pure being or absolute being is not denied of God in the *Parisian Questions,* for he is said to contain all perfections in their purity and fullness.[84]

One does not have to read far in Eckhart to realize that he loved paradox and contradiction. For him, as for Nicholas of Cusa, the compatibility of contradictories was necessary for the ascent to mystical theology.[85] Though the truth he saw was simple, he could express it only in contradictory and paradoxical language. In the *Parisian Questions* he dissociates and opposes intelligence and being, denying being to God in order to emphasize the divine transcendence over creatures. The stance he adopts in this work is an ascending one: he looks upward to God from the perspective of creatures and sees him as pure intelligence devoid of the being that he creates. In the *Opus Tripartitum* he no longer opposes intelligence and being in God: he is now seen to be pure being and creatures to be nothing in themselves. Their only being is that of God in whom they exist. Eckhart's stance in this work is now a descending one: he looks at creatures from the divine perspective and sees them in their pure nothingness.[86]

Both of these viewpoints on God and being are present in a sermon dating from the period of the *Parisian Questions* (1302-1303):

> Ignorant masters say that God is pure being; he is as high above being as the highest angel is above a midge. If I call God a being it would be just as wrong as to call the sun pale or black. God is

84 *Ibid.*

85 See Nicholas of Cusa, *Apologia Doctae Ignorantiae, Opera Omnia* (Leipzig, 1932) 2, p. 6.

86 See V. Lossky, *op. cit.*, pp. 217-220.

> neither this nor that [i.e., he is not limited or finite] .... But if I said that God is not a being and that he is above being, I did not by so doing deny being to God. On the contrary, I enhanced it in him. If I take copper alloyed with gold, it is still there, but in a higher manner than it is in itself .... When we apprehend God as being, we apprehend him in his antechamber, for being is the antechamber in which he dwells. Where is he then in his temple, in which he, the Holy One, shines? Reason is the temple of God. God dwells nowhere more properly than in his temple, in reason, as the second master said: 'God is an intellect which lives in the knowledge of itself alone.' He dwells in himself alone, where nothing has ever troubled him, because he is there alone in his stillness. In his knowledge of himself God knows himself in himself.[87]

While affirming being of God, Eckhart never forgets that intellect is a superior divine name, nor that unity is a still higher name. Indeed, in his trinitarian doctrine he appropriates unity and intellect for the Father, life for the Son, and being for the Holy Spirit. In the divine emanations of the trinitarian life of God being comes last; but it is there in the Godhead. Beyond the distinction of the divine persons is the unity of the divine nature which transcends the trinity. In that unity "every distinction is alien to God, whether in nature or in persons."[88]

Thus many names may be given to God, but in the last analysis he is unnameable. He has a name that is above every

87 *Sermon 17*, transl. by J. M. Clark, *Meister Eckhart* (London, etc. 1957), pp. 206-208.

88 Condemned proposition 15; see G. Théry, *op. cit.*, I, p. 167, n. 15, with Eckhart's reply, p. 191, n. 15. "There is no distinction in either the divine nature or persons. Proof: nature itself is one and this is one. Any person is one: the very one that nature itself is. Whatever a person is, three persons are likewise the same one." Blakney, *op. cit.*, p. 275, n. 15.

name, and that Eckhart paradoxically calls 'The Unnameable.'[89] A wonderful name indeed that cannot be known or pronounced! God revealed his name as 'being' when he said to Moses 'I am who am', but at the same time — and more profoundly in Eckhart's view — he concealed his name, for the very nature of God is to be hidden being (*esse absconditum*).[90]

Eckhart, like all mystics, experienced God in a realm beyond the conceptual knowledge of metaphysics or speculative theology. His encounter with God is best expressed in negative terms, as in the following passage from a sermon:

> God is without name, for no one can say or understand anything of him .... If I say: 'God is good', this is not true. I am good, but God is not good .... If I say further: 'God is wise', this is not true, I am wiser than he. If I say also: 'God is a being', this is not true; he is a being above being and a superessential negation. A master says: 'If I had a God whom I could know, I would not think him to be God.' ... You must love him as he is: neither God, nor spirit, nor person, nor image; rather the One without mixture, pure and luminous.[91]

What else is Eckhart doing here but expressing in Neoplatonic terms an experience shared by all Christian mystics, that their encounter with God takes place in silence and stillness beyond all conceptual thought and language? Aquinas voices the same experience when he says: "Man reaches the peak of his knowledge of God when he realizes that he does not know him,

89 *LW*, I, pp. 95-96, nn. 298-300. The source of the expression *nomen innominabile* is Dionysius, *De Divinis Nominibus*, I, 6; PG 3, 596. On this point see the profound remarks of V. Lossky, *op. cit.*, p. 18.

90 *LW*, *ibid.*

91 Sermo 99. *Meister Eckhart*, transl. by C. de B. Evans, p. 246. I have used the translation of Hilda Graef in J. Ancelet-Hustache, *Master Eckhart and the Rhineland Mystics*, p. 55.

understanding that the divine reality surpasses all human conceptions of it.'"[92] Does this not suggest that however divergent their metaphysics and speculative theologies may be, these two sons of St. Dominic were at one in their personal experience of God?

When listing arguments or statements, Eckhart usually numbers them, but occasionally he does not. For the sake of clarity and consistency I have added numbers in the latter cases.

92 St. Thomas, *In I Sent.*, d. 8, q. 1, a. 1, ad 4; ed. Mandonnet, I, pp. 196-197; *De Potentia*, VII, 5, ad 14; *In Dionysii De Divinis Nominibus*, VII, 4, 432. See J. Owens, "Aquinas — 'Darkness of Ignorance' in the Most Refined Notion of God," *Soutwestern Journal of Philosophy* 5 (1974), 93-110.

I

PARISIAN QUESTIONS

Question 1

Are Existence and Understanding the Same in God?

I reply that they are the same in reality, and perhaps both in reality and in thought.

First I offer proofs I have seen. Five are in the *Contra Gentiles*[1] and the sixth is in the First Part [of the *Summa Theologiae*].[2] All are based on the fact that God is the first and simple being; for something cannot be the first being if it is not simple.

1. First proof: Understanding is an immanent act, and whatever is in the first being is the first being. Hence God is his act of understanding, and he is also his existence. The conclusion follows.

2. There is no accident in God. Hence his existence is the same as his essence. It follows that because God's act of understanding is identical with God and with his essence, it is also identical with his existence. The conclusion follows.

3. Nothing is more perfect than the first being. Now second act is related to the intellect as the soul's wakefulness to sleep, and this is something more perfect than first act. It follows that the act of understanding is the existence itself of God.

1 St. Thomas, *Contra Gentiles*, I, 45, nn. 2-6.

2 St. Thomas, *Summa Theologiae*, I, 14, 4.

4. In God there is no passive potentiality. But there would be unless understanding and existence were the same in God.

5. Everything exists for the sake of its operation. If, then, God's act of understanding were different from his existence, we would have to grant that God has an end other than himself and his essence. This cannot be, for the end is a cause, and we cannot grant that God has a cause. The same conclusion follows from the fact that the first being is infinite, and the infinite has no end.

6. The act of understanding is related to the [intelligible] species as existence is related to essence. Now the divine essence takes the place of an intelligible species. Consequently, God's existence being identical with his essence, all of these are entirely the same in him.

Second, I show this by a method I employed elsewhere.[3] Though 'man' and 'rational' are convertible terms, it is not because he is rational that he is a man, but rather because he is a man that he is rational. Now it is certain that if existence were perfect, all [perfections] would be had through that existence: life and understanding and every kind of operation. Nothing else would have to be added in order to exercise any operation. For example, if fire could do everything through its form, that is to say both exist and heat, the form of fire, through which it could do them, would be capable of all these [operations]; there would be no addition or composition. Now God's existence is most excellent and perfect, being the primary actuality and the perfection of all things, bringing all acts to completion, so that if it were removed everything would be reduced to nothing. So God does everything through his existence, both interiorly in the

3 This work of Eckhart has not been identified.

Godhead and exteriorly in creatures, in each, however, in its own way. Thus in God existence itself is his act of understanding, for he acts and knows through his existence.

Third, I declare that it is not my present opinion that God understands because he exists, but rather that he exists because he understands. God is an intellect and understanding, and his understanding itself is the ground of his existence. It is said in John 1: "In the beginning was the Word, and the Word was with God, and the Word was God."[4] The Evangelist did not say: "In the beginning was being, and God was being." A word is completely related to an intellect, where it is either the speaker or what is spoken, and not existence or a composite being. Our Savior also says in John 14, "I am the Truth."[5] Truth has reference to an intellect, implying or containing a relation [to it]; and a relation owes its whole existence to a mind; and as such it is a real category. Similarly time owes its whole existence to a mind, and yet it is a species of the real category of quantity. Hence "I am the Truth." Augustine comments on this statement in his book *On the Trinity,* VIII, 2.[6] So truth, like a word, clearly has reference to an intellect.

After the text of John 1 quoted above there follows: "All things were made through him."[7] This should be read, "All things that were made through him, exist," so that existence itself comes to creatures afterward. Thus the author of the *Book of Causes* says, "The first of created things is existence."[8] Hence as

4 John 1, 1.

5 John 14, 6.

6 St. Augustine, *De Trinitate*, VIII, 2, 3; CCL 50, pp. 270-271.

7 John 1, 3. Eckhart's interpretation is achieved by inserting a comma in John's text. "Omnia per ipsum facta sunt" then reads: "Omnia per ipsum facta, sunt."

8 *Liber de Causis*, prop. 4; ed. Bardenhewer (Freiburg, Switz., 1882), p. 166. This work is based on Proclus' *Elements of Theology*; it was translated into Latin in the twelfth century.

soon as we come to existence we come to a creature. Existence, then, has primarily the nature of something creatable. This is why some writers say that the existence of a creature is related to God only as to an efficient cause, whereas its essence is related to him as to an exemplar cause.[9] Wisdom, on the contrary, having reference to an intellect, does not have the nature of something creatable. If you reply that it does, for it is written [of wisdom] in Ecclesiasticus 24, "From the beginning and before all ages I have been created,"[10] 'created' can be interpreted to mean 'begotten'. But I interpret this differently: "From the beginning and before created ages, I am." So God, who is the creator and is not creatable, is an intellect and understanding; he is not being or existence.

In order to clarify this, my first claim is that understanding is superior to existence and belongs to a different order. We all say that "The work of nature is the work of an intelligence."[11] If this is so, every mover is either intelligent or it can be traced back to a mind that directs it in its movement. It follows that the possessor of a mind is more perfect than something that does not possess one; as in the process of becoming what is imperfect comes first, so that the analysis concludes with an intellect or intelligent being as that which is highest and most perfect. Therefore understanding is superior to existence.

Some say that existence, life, and intelligence can be viewed in two ways: 1) in themselves, and then existence is first, life second, and intelligence third; 2) in relation to that which participates in them, and then intelligence is first, life second, and

9 Henry of Ghent, *Quodlibet* X, q. 7 (Paris, 1518), fol. 418v.

10 Ecclesiasticus 24, 14.

11 See St. Thomas, *De Potentia*, 1, 5. This saying is based on Aristotle, *De Generatione Animalium*, I, 23, 731a 24.

existence third.[12] But I believe the exact opposite to be true. For "In the beginning was the Word,"[13] which is entirely related to an intellect. Consequently, among perfections intelligence comes first and then being or existence.

My second claim is that understanding itself, and whatever has to do with intellect, belong to a different order than existence. As the *Metaphysics* III, says, finality and goodness have no place in mathematics;[14] consequently neither does being, because being is the same as the good. The *Metaphysics* VI also says, "Good and evil are in things, and truth and falsity are in the mind."[15] There it is also said that truth, which is in the mind, is not a being, just as accidental being is not a being, because it has no cause, as we read in the same passage. Hence, a being existing in the mind, as it exists in the mind, does not have the nature of being; as such, it inclines to the opposite of existence. An image, as such, is also not a being: the more we think about its entity the more it distracts us from knowing the thing whose image it is. Similarly, as I have said elsewhere,[16] if a [cognitive] species existing in the soul had the nature of being, by its means we would not know the thing whose likeness it is: if it had the nature of being, as such it would make us know itself and distract us from knowing the thing whose likeness it is. Thus, whatever is related to the intellect as such is not a being. We can think about things God could not do, as when we think about fire without considering its heat; but God could not produce fire that did not heat.

12 See Dionysius, *De Divinis Nominibus*, V, 5; PG 3, 820. See also St. Augustine, *De Libero Arbitrio*, II, 3, n. 7; PL 32, 1243-1244. Eckhart here differs from St. Thomas, *Summa Theol.* I-II, 2, 5; I, 4, 2, ad 3; *In Dionys. De Divinis Nominibus*, c. 5, lect. 1; ed. C. Pera (Rome, 1950), pp. 235-6; nn. 634-5.

13 John 1, 1.

14 Aristotle, *Metaph.* II, 2, 996a 27 ff.

15 *Ibid.*, VI, 4, 1027b 25.

16 See below, p. 53.

My third claim is that here the imagination fails. For our knowledge is different from God's. His knowledge is the cause of things whereas our knowledge is caused by them. Consequently, because our knowledge is dependent upon the being by which it is caused, with equal reason being itself is dependent upon God's knowledge. Hence everything in God transcends existence and is totally understanding.

On the basis of this I show that in God there is no being or existence. Nothing is formally in both a cause and its effect if the cause is a true cause.[17] Now God is the cause of all existence. It follows that existence is not formally present in God. Of course if you wish to call understanding existence I do not mind. Nevertheless I say that if there is anything in God that you want to call existence, it belongs to him through his understanding.

Again, a principle is never the same as that which follows from a principle, as a point is never a line. Now God is the principle or cause of existence or being itself; hence he is not the being or existence of his creature. Nothing in the creature is in God except as in its cause, and it is not there formally. Consequently, since existence belongs to creatures, it is not in God except as in its cause. Threfore existence is not in God but purity of existence. When someone who wants to conceal his identity and name is asked at night "Who are you?" he replies, "I am who I am." So the Lord, wishing to show that he possesses purity of existence, said "I am who I am."[18] He did not say simply "I am," but added "who I am." Therefore existence does not befit God, unless you call this purity existence.

17 For the notion of a 'true cause' see below, p. 54. The origin of the notion is Dionysius, *De Coelesti Hierarchia*, c. 2, n. 3; PG 3, 140 C.

18 Exodus 3, 14.

Moreover, a stone in potentiality is not a stone, nor is a stone in its cause a stone. Therefore a being in its cause is not a being. If follows that because God is the universal cause of being, nothing in him has the nature of being; rather it has the nature of intellect and understanding, to which it is not essential to have a cause, as it is essential that being be caused. And all things are contained in the power of intelligence itself as in their highest cause.

Again, if several things are named by analogy, what is formally in one of the analogates is not [formally] in the other.[19] For instance, health formally exists only in an animal; in a diet or urine there is no more health than in a stone. Now all creatures are formally beings; hence God will not be formally a being. As I have said elsewhere,[20] we speak of accidents in relation to substance, which is formally being and to which existence formally attaches; hence accidents are not beings nor do they give existence to substance. An accident, however, is a quantity or a quality, and it gives quantified or qualified existence: extended, long or short, white or black; but it does not give existence, nor is it a being.

It is not valid to argue: An accident is produced in a qualified sense of the term 'production'; therefore it is a being in a qualified sense. I assert that it is not produced even in a qualified sense. I was taught that a production absolutely speaking occurs when a more formal substance is produced from a less formal substance, while a production in a qualified sense occurs when the opposite happens. I was not taught that when

19 For Eckhart's doctrine of analogy, see V. Lossky, *Théologie négative et connaissance de Dieu chez Maître Eckhart* (Paris, 1960), pp. 286-337. Also J. Koch, "Zur Analogielehre Meister Eckharts," *Mélanges offerts à Etienne Gilson* (Toronto-Paris, 1959), 327-350.

20 See *In Exodum*, *LW*, II, p. 58, n. 54.

something is changed from one accident to another this is called a production in a qualified sense, but an alteration. So I do not deny to accidents what belongs to them, nor do I wish to grant to them what does not belong to them.

I also assert that existence does not belong to God, nor is he a being, but he is something loftier than being. Aristotle says that the power of sight must be colorless so that it can perceive all colors, and that the intellect is not a natural form so that it can know all forms.[21] So also I deny existence itself and suchlike of God so that he may be the cause of all existence and precontain all things. Thus, as I do not deny to God anything that is his, so I do deny to him what is not his. These negations, as Damascene says in the first book [of *On Orthodox Faith*], signify in God an excess of affirmation.[22] So I deny nothing to God that is his by nature, asserting as I do that God precontains everything in purity, fullness, and perfection, more abundantly and extensively, because he is the ground and cause of all things. And this is what he intended to say when he declared "I am who am."[23]

Eckhart

21 Aristotle, *De Anima*, II, 7, 418b 26-27; III, 4, 429a 24.

22 St. John Damascene, *De Fide Orthodoxa*, I, 4; ed. M. Buytaert (St. Bonaventure, New York, 1955), p. 21, n. 5.

23 Exodus 3, 14.

Question 2
Is an Angel's Understanding, as Denoting an Action, the Same as his Existence?

I reply that it is not.

Some demonstrate this well, in the following manner:[1]. Every action is either transient or immanent. Now existence is not a transient action, for this sort of action goes outward, whereas existence remains within. Neither is existence an immanent action, like understanding or sensation, for this kind of action is unlimited, either absolutely, as in the case of understanding, or relatively, as in the case of sensation. Existence, on the contrary, is limited and determined to a genus and species.

But I have other ways of proving this.

1. The intellect, as an intellect, is none of the things it knows; it must be "unmixed with anything," "having nothing in common," so that it might know everything, as the *De Anima* III says.[2] Similarly, sight must be colorless so that it can see all colors. If the intellect, therefore, insofar as it is an intellect, is nothing, it follows that neither is understanding some existence.

2. An action and power, insofar as it is a power, have their existence from their object, for an object is like a subject.[3] Now a subject gives existence to that of which it is the subject. Hence an object will also give existence to that of which it is the object, namely to a power and an action. Now the object is exterior, while existence is something interior. Consequently, the act of

1 See St. Thomas, *Summa Theol.* I, 54, 2.

2 Aristotle, *De Anima*, II, 7, 418b 26 ff.

3 Eckhart is likely thinking of Aquinas' analogy between an object and a subject: "A subject is related to a science as an object is related to a power or habit." *Summa Theol.* I, 1, 7. See St. Thomas, *De Veritate*, 8, 6, ad 8.

understanding, which is caused by an object, and similarly a power, as such, are not a being nor do they have any existence.

3. A [cognitive] likeness is the principle of the operations of the senses and intellect. Now a [cognitive] likeness is in no sense a being. Consequently, neither will understanding nor sensation be in any sense a being, for an action has no more entity than a [cognitive] likeness or form, which is the principle of the action. I prove that a [cognitive] likeness, which is the principle of the act of understanding, is in no sense a being as follows: Being in the mind is contradistinguished to the being divided into the ten categories, and also to substance and accident, as is shown in the *Metaphysics* VI.[4] But what is contradistinguished to substance and accident is not a being. So a being in the mind is not a being. Now a [cognitive] likeness is a being in the mind. The conclusion follows.

4. If a [cognitive] likeness were a being it would be an accident, for it is not a substance. But a [cognitive] likeness is not an accident, for an accident has a subject that gives it existence. Now a [cognitive] likeness has an object but not a subject. Place and subject are not the same. A [cognitive] likeness is in the soul, not as in a subject but as in a place; for the soul is the "place of [cognitive] likenesses" — not the whole soul but the intellect.[5] It is clear that the soul would be the subject of a [cognitive] likeness if it had a subject. Consequently, a [cognitive] likeness is not a being.

5. If a [cognitive] likeness or act of understanding were a being, it could be known by a creature; but this is false.

6. If the [cognitive] likeness of a man were a being, it would be either the being that man is or a being that is not man. But

4 Aristotle, *Metaph.* VI, 2, 1026a 33.
5 Aristotle, *De Anima*, III, 4, 429a 27.

clearly it is not the being that man is; and similarly it is not a being that is not man, because then it would not be the principle whereby man is known. Consequently it is not a being. Anything made to serve a purpose is made to suit that purpose. Thus, because a saw is made for cutting it is not made from a different material for a king or for a carpenter. Now the purpose of a [cognitive] likeness is to represent something to the intellect. Hence it should be such as to better represent that thing, and it represents it better if it is not a being than if it were a being. In fact, if it were a being it would detract from its representative function. Consequently it is not a being — unless you call it a being in the mind.

Knowledge is a quality and a true, though potential, being: it has the being of a habit. Thus knowledge belongs rather on the side of the subject, which is something interior, whereas the intellect and the [cognitive] likeness belong on the side of the object, which is something exterior. Consequently, existence being something interior, these have no existence.

7. The intellect, as such, is neither here, nor now, nor a definite thing. But every being or existence is in a definite genus and species. So the intellect, as such, is not a being, nor does it have an existence. It follows that it will not cause the act of understanding to be a being, for an action has no more existence than the doer of the action; in fact it has less.

You may say that if the intellect is neither here, nor now, nor some definite thing it is absolutely nothing. My reply is that the intellect is a natural power of the soul. Consequently it is something, for the soul is a true being, and it is the source of the true being of its natural powers.

8. Being and good are convertible terms. But we do not find in the intellect the nature of the good or of efficient or final

causality. This is clear from the *Metaphysics* III.[6] As is said there, none of these are found in abstract mathematical entities, because as such they exist only in the intellect. So the intellect does not have the nature of being; and consequently understanding, as denoting an action, is not a being.

9. A universal is not a being. Now a universal is produced through an act of understanding. Consequently, neither will the act of understanding, which produces the universal, be a being.

10. A being is some definite thing. This is why a genus is not a being, for it is something indeterminate. Now the intellect and the act of understanding are something indeterminate; therefore they are not a being.

11. A being, as present in its cause, is not a being; for nothing univocal has the true nature of a cause. It follows that the nature of being is on a lower level than its cause. So we find the nature of being in that which is on a lower level. This is why we do not find the nature of being in God, for all things descend from him. It follows that because our act of understanding is caused by being it is on a lower level than being, and thus it tends toward non-being; nor does it have existence.

Thus it is clear that the angel's understanding, as denoting an action, is not his existence.

The Dominican Eckhart

6 Aristotle, *Metaph.* II, 2, 996a 27.

Question 3

A Question of Master Gonsalvo [of Spain],[1] *containing the Arguments of Master Eckhart*

Is the Praise of God in Heaven more Excellent than the Love of Him on Earth?

Arguments for the affirmative:

1. What is nearer and closer to God and unites us more directly to God is more excellent. This is the case with praise in heaven in comparison with love on earth. Hence the conclusion follows.

2. The act of what is more perfect is itself more perfect. But the praise of God in heaven is an act of those who are more perfect, for it is an act of the blessed, whereas love on earth is an act of those who are unhappy, because they are pilgrims on earth.

3. What has the nature of an end is more excellent than what has the nature of a means to an end. Now the act of understanding has the nature of an end, whereas love has the nature of a tendency toward an end: love seems to mean nothing but an inclining toward something.

4. An act produced by God is more excellent than an act produced by the will. Now the vision of God in heaven is caused directly by God, while the love of God — even in heaven — is produced by the will. Hence the conclusion follows. This argument is confirmed by the fact that the action of a more perfect and powerful agent is itself more perfect. But God is a more perfect agent than the will.

1 Gonsalvus Hispanus. See below, p. 11.

Solution

I reply:

1. If love on earth and praise in heaven are considered just in themselves and in their essential natures, love on earth is more excellent than praise in heaven, indeed than vision in heaven. For that act is absolutely more excellent than another which any right will, needing nothing, would prefer to another. I say 'needing nothing' because when we are in need we choose a lesser good in preference to a greater good, as one in need would rather earn money than philosophize, as is said in the *Ethics*.[2] Now a right will, in need of nothing, would choose the love of God on earth in preference to the vision of God in heaven, because that will is by no means right which prefers a finite and lesser good to an infinite and greater good. This would be the case if one chose the vision of God in heaven in preference to the love of God on earth, for he would love something other than God, namely the vision of God, more than God, and he would prefer it to him, because one who loves the vision of God more than the love of him would rather be without the love than the vision. But one who is willing to be without the love of God does not love God. Hence one who prefers the vision of God to love of him would rather be without God than the vision of God. So he wills or loves the vision of God more than God. It follows that one cannot prefer the vision of God to love of him without loving the vision of God more than God. This kind of will is not right. But if one prefers the love of God to the vision of him, it does not follow that he prefers anything other than God to God. Consequently to a right will the love of God on earth is more excellent than the vision of God in heaven.

2 The correct reference is to Aristotle, *Topics*, III, 4, 118a 10-11.

2. If there are two things of the same [kind] and one of them is absolutely more perfect than some [third] thing, the other will also be more perfect than the [third] thing.[3] Now love on earth and in heaven belong to the same species, and love in heaven is more perfect than vision in heaven. For nothing is more excellent than happiness; so that in which happiness more fully resides is more excellent. Now the happiness of heaven consists in the love of God more than in the vision of him, for happiness is found primarily in that which distinguishes it more from its opposite, which is unhappiness. But what distinguishes happiness from unhappiness is love rather than vision or knowledge, for the state of unhappiness opposed to the happiness of heaven is not some state on earth but the state of damnation. The blessed have a right state of mind along with the act of understanding, and similarly they have a right state of will along with the act of loving. As for the damned, they have in many respects a right condition of mind but they lack a right will. It follows that because the blessed share with the damned rightness of mind but in no way rightness of will, love rather than vision distinguishes the blessed from the damned. Consequently, love is a more important feature in happiness than vision; so it is more excellent. It also follows that love on earth is more excellent than vision in heaven.

3. As Aristotle says in the *Posterior Analytics*,[4] that is better whose opposite is worse. The opposite of love on earth, which is hatred of God, is worse than the opposite of the praise of God in heaven, which is blasphemy in hell, because hatred of God on earth is a sin of malice and it is the extreme in malice, whereas blasphemy in hell comes from ignorance. But a sin of ignorance

3 See *ibid.*, III, 2, 117b 33-38.

4 Aristotle, *Posterior Analytics*, II, 6, 92a 21.

is not as great as a sin of malice, nor is ignorance as bad as malice. Therefore the conclusion follows.

4. If one species excels another in its essentials, each individual in the species that excels absolutely surpasses every individual in the inferior species,[5] though it can be excelled in a particular respect. For example, the human species in its essentials excels the species of lion, so every man absolutely excels every individual lion, though he can be surpassed in a particular respect, as in speed of running, boldness of spirit, and strength of body. Now love on earth in its essentials excels the vision of heaven, for the essential factors entering into love and vision are power, habit, and object. But the power, habit, and object of love on earth are more excellent, absolutely speaking, than the power, habit, [and object] of vision in heaven, as was shown above.[6] Therefore every individual act of love on earth will be more perfect than every individual act of vision in heaven. Now the praise [of God] in heaven is an individual act of vision in heaven. Therefore the conclusion follows.

Arguments of Eckhart [for the Negative Side]

Against this position some authors present the following arguments to show that the intellect, its act, and its habit are more excellent than the will, its act, and its habit.[7]

1. That power, act, or habit is more excellent whose object is simpler, higher, and prior. Now the object of the intellect and its habit and act, which is being, is more primary, simpler, and loftier than the object of the will, which is the good, for the whole

5 See Aristotle, *Topics*, III, 2, 117b 33-38.
6 See above, p. 56.
7 See St. Thomas, *Summa Theol.* I, 82, 3.

nature of the good is existence itself. Hence the conclusion follows.

2. That power is more excellent whose habits are more excellent. The acquired intellectual habits, namely wisdom, understanding, and prudence, which are in the intellect, are more excellent than the acquired moral virtues, which reside in the appetitive powers. The conclusion follows.

3. That power is more perfect whose act is more perfect. Now understanding, the act of the intellect, is more perfect than the act of the will, for understanding proceeds by way of purification and reaches the bare entity of a thing.[8]

4. Understanding is a sort of conformity to God or deification, for God is understanding itself and not existence.[9]

5. Understanding, as such, is something subsistent.

6. It is, as such, uncreatable.[10] A box, existing in thought, is not creatable. Now these are not characteristics of love. The conclusion follows.

7. That is better which is the exact reason why we are pleasing to God. This is understanding: one is pleasing to God precisely because he understands,[11] for if knowledge is taken away absolutely nothing is left.

8. That power is more excellent in which freedom resides. Now it resides first and foremost in the intellect,[12] for something is free if it is unencumbered by matter, as is clear in the case of

8 See *Sermo XXIV*, 2; *LW* 4, n. 247; *The Book of Divine Comfort*, 3; transl. by R. Blakney, *Meister Eckhart* (New York-London, 1941), pp. 72-3.

9 See above, p. 45.

10 See *Sermo XXIX*; *LW* 4, nn. 295-305.

11 According to Eckhart sanctifying grace is in the intellect as in a subject. See *Comm. in Sap.*; ed. G. Théry, "Le commentaire de Maître Eckhart sur le livre de la sagesse," *Archives d'histoire doctrinale et littéraire du moyen âge*, 4 (1929), 361-2.

12 See G. Théry, "Edition critique des pièces relatives au procès d'Eckhart ...," p. 225, n. 21.

the senses. The intellect and the act of understanding are most unencumbered by matter, because the less reflexive something is the more material it is. Now the power of reflection resides not in being but in understanding, as when by understanding that which is identical with itself reflects upon itself.

9. Gregory of Nyssa, in his book *De Anima*, chapters 39 and 40, says that freedom moves from reason down to the will.[13]

Moreover, something is free because it can act in different ways. The will can act in different ways only as a consequence of reason and through reason.

Again, choice is a conclusion following upon deliberation, which is an act of the intellect. So the ground of freedom is in the intellect. Thus freedom resides primarily and originally in the intellect, though it is formally in the will.

10. The good and the best, or the end, are the object of the will. So a thing is best because it has the nature of the best. It follows that that is better in which the nature of the best is to be found. Now something has the nature of the best because of existence itself, for if existence is taken away there is nothing. Consequently existence, which is the object of the intellect, is better that the best, which is the object of the will.

Moreover, the nature of the best resides in the intellect because the nature of truth is in the intellect, and the nature of truth is the nature of the best. Silver, for example, is good and the best because it is true [silver]. If you deprive the best of its nature it is nothing. Hence the nature of the best is found on the side of the intellect and its object. It follows that something is best because it is in the intellect. Being in the intellect it moves away from the good toward the nature of the best, and there it

13 This work is not by Gregory but by Nemesius. See his *De Natura Hominis*, c. 41; transl. Alfano; ed. C. Burkhard (Leipzig, 1917), p. 132. The exact text is not there.

becomes conformed to God and approaches its cause. So the nature of the best is on the side of the intellect rather than on the side of the will. It follows that the object of the intellect is more excellent, loftier, and more primary than the object of the will, and that the intellect is more excellent than the will itself.

11. Again, that is freer and more excellent which moves in a nobler way. Now the intellect moves in a more excellent manner, for it is more perfect to move as an end[14] — the end being the cause of causes. This is clear from *Physics* VII.[15] Consequently even God moves as the object of desire, as is said in *Metaphysics* XII.[16] But the intellect moves as an end, the will as an efficient cause.

Moreover, the intellect with its objects moves as the reason for moving, while the will moves as a mover.[17]

[Gonsalvo's] Refutation of Eckhart's Arguments for the Superiority of the Intellect over the Will

1. To the first argument I reply that it does not follow that because something is prior and simpler it is more perfect. Indeed, the contrary is often true in creatures, as is clear in the case of universals.

2. I reply to the second argument that there are eminent writers who say that the moral virtues are more excellent than

14 See Eckhart's *Apology* in G. Théry, *art. cit.*, p. 204, n. 12.

15 Aristotle, *Physics*, II, 3, 195a 24.

16 Aristotle, *Metaph.*, XII, 7, 1072b 3.

17 See St. Thomas, *De Veritate*, 22, 12: "Two things are to be taken into account in any action, the agent and the reason for acting. In heating, the agent is fire and the reason for acting is heat. Similarly in moving, the end is said to move as the reason for moving, but the efficient cause, as the one producing the movement, that is, the one which brings the subject of the motion from potency to act."

the intellectual virtues. Cicero, for one, in *De Officiis* 2, claims that justice is more perfect than prudence.[18]

The argument is defective in another respect. We should prove the excellence of perfections on the basis of the excellence of the highest perfections. A perfection that is not the highest, such as clearness of sight, can indeed be greater in brute animals than in men. But the highest perfection of man is more excellent than the highest perfection of animals, and for this reason man is more excellent than any animal. Now it is not the acquired but the infused virtues that are the highest perfections of the intellect and will. It follows that the power is absolutely speaking more excellent in which the highest infused perfection, namely love, resides. This is the will. So the argument falls down.

The argument is defective in still another way. It presupposes that love is not absolutely more perfect, though more excellent from the point of view of merit. This is invalid, for to be better in the sight of God is not a qualification that lessens value. So we can reason: Something is better in the sight of God and from the perspective of merit; hence it is absolutely better. This is true of love.

3. When, thirdly, it is said that understanding analyzes [its objects] into their deepest elements, I reply that this indeed proves that the intellect holds the highest rank among cognitive powers, and the statement is true. I also claim that the will occupies the loftiest position among appetitive powers. But this does not prove the superiority of the intellect over the will. Just as the intellect proceeds in two different ways, by discovering and by analyzing [objects] into their smallest elements, so there is a corresponding twofold procedure on the part of the will.

18 Cicero, *De Officiis*, II, c. 9, 34 (Leipzig, 1908), p. 68.

4. To the fourth argument I reply that love deifies one more than understanding. A sign of this is the fact that the highest order of angels takes its name from love: it is called Seraphim from the fire of love.[19] When it is added that God is understanding and not existence, I retort that God is not existence in the way we understand and express it, as we see existence in things, but God is existence itself as far as the reality signified is concerned. To say the contrary clearly contradicts the saints and Scripture: "Truly I say to you: before Abraham was made, I am,"[20] and "He alone is."[21] In expounding this text Gregory says in *Moralia* 16 that everything would sink into nothingness unless the hand of the creator upheld it.[22]

5-6. To the fifth and sixth arguments I reply that when it is said that understanding is subsistent and uncreatable, this is true of the divine understanding but not of a creature's understanding. A box and suchlike existing in thought are creatable. Intellectual natures are also supremely creatable; otherwise they could not be brought into existence. They are created from the same matter from which all other creatures are produced, as Augustine clearly says in the beginning of his *De Genesi contra Manichaeos*.[23]

7. I reply to the seventh argument that when the claim is made that one is pleasing to God precisely because he understands, this is a strange statement indeed. Taking knowledge as separate from love, it is false. When it is said, If knowledge is taken away nothing is left, this does not follow. According to

19 See Hugh of St. Victor, *Comm. in Dionys. De Cael. Hier.*, 6; PL 175, 1035 C.
20 John 8, 58.
21 Job 23, 13.
22 Gregory the Great, *Libri Moralium*, XVI, c. 37, n. 45; PL 75, 1143.
23 St. Augustine, *De Genesi contra Manichaeos*, I, c. 5-7, nn. 9-11; PL 34, 178.

Aristotle's *Topics*,[24] when treating of contradictory terms an inference is not valid in itself but when the terms are converted; otherwise no conclusion follows. It is invalid to argue: If imagination is removed, understanding ceases; therefore imagination is better than understanding. So too it does not follow that if quantity is removed and action ceases, therefore quantity is the main cause of action.

Moreover, as is commonly said, a statement true in itself is true in all cases. Consequently, if one is pleasing to God precisely because he understands, every knower would be pleasing to God. This is plainly false from the words of the Apostle: "Thus there is no excuse for them."[25] Again, if a person were pleasing to God precisely because he understands, one who knows more would be more pleasing, and one who knows most would be most pleasing. This is false: there are many ordinary men and women more pleasing to God than the well educated. Moreover, that is not the precise cause of something which is compatible with its opposite. But knowledge is compatible with the opposite of being pleasing.

8. Replying to the eighth argument, I can deny its assertion about freedom: that immateriality is the cause of freedom. As I have said elsewhere,[26] I am more inclined to believe that angels and souls are composed of matter and form than that they are simple beings. But granted that what is free is immaterial, it is not enough to be immaterial to be free, for then a habit of an immaterial power would be free, which is not the case. Furthermore, both the intellect and will are immaterial, so this argument proves the freedom of the will as much as it proves the freedom of the intellect.

24 Aristotle, *Topics*, II, 22, 113b 15-26.

25 Romans 1, 20.

26 *Conclusiones Metaphysicae*, IX, concl. 29, in Duns Scotus, *Opera Omnia*, ed. Vivès, VI (Paris, 1892), p. 629.

9. To the ninth argument I reply: The statement is true that the will cannot be inclined to different things unless they are known. But from this it does not follow that freedom resides only in the [power] that knows these different things. This is a fallacy of the consequent.

Regarding Gregory of Nyssa, I reply that these words are not to be found there but rather the following: "Everyone who deliberates weighs what he ought to do, with the choice remaining with him."[27] And further on: "[Man has] free will because he is rational."[28] I assert that this is true if 'rational' expresses the definition of an essence and not of a power.

10. When it is said that something has the nature of the best from the intellect, for truth is the nature of the best, I reply: If it is thought that truth is the nature of the best in the sense that the nature of the one is the cause of the other, or that truth is the cause of the best, it is false. It is also false that the nature of the two is the same. But if it is thought that the two go together, this is true, for one cannot exist without the other. But from this nothing can be concluded for the present question. Nor is it true that something has the nature of the best because it is known.

11. When it is said that the intellect moves as an end, this is false. Knowledge is an essential requirement for the movement of the will, but it does not move as an end, for then knowledge would be the essential and primary object of desire, which is false. Some desirable reality moves as an end, though it could not move unless it were previously known. The activity of the intellect is essentially needed for the movements of the will and it is their essential cause, not in the sense that it impresses [something on the will] but that it cooperates [with the will] in

27 Nemesius, *De Natura Hominis*, c. 41, 5, p. 132, lines 3-6.
28 *Ibid.*, c. 41, 7, p. 132, line 17.

the following way: In order for an agent to act upon a patient the agent must draw near to the patient; without this nearness the agent would not have a sufficient causality for acting, though it is not [this nearness] but the form of the agent that is the cause eliciting the act. The present case is similar. Knowledge is like nearness: through knowledge the object becomes present; and just as it is not the nearness but the form of the agent that is the cause eliciting the act, so the knowledge is not the cause that produces the act but the will itself.

Replies to the Main Arguments

1. To the first argument I reply that a closer and more direct union does not prove the greater excellence of an act unless it is combined with the more excellent nature of a power.

2. To the second argument I reply that praise is not an essential but an accidental act of the blessed. Nor are persons on earth as such unhappy: one is made unhappy by his own will.

3. I reply to the third argument that love, in the present context, means an inclination to God. But it is more perfect to incline toward God than to be the terminus of the movement of something else, as is the case with understanding.

4. To the fourth argument I reply that each power brings forth its act within itself. Granted that the will also brings forth its act within itself, and that God produces vision in the intellect, still the argument is invalid, for the will's eliciting its act in itself does not exclude God's producing the same act as the principal cause.

And even if God were not operative in a special way in the act of the will, the proof is still invalid. It is true that an act produced by a higher agent is more excellent if the agent operates with its whole power. If it does not, this is not necessary. Now God does not operate with his whole power when he causes the beatific vision; but the will does elicit its act with its whole power.

Furthermore, the fact that something is more passive does not take away from the excellence of the patient unless the undergoing [of the action] entails the removal of a contrary. Now, to be more passive regarding the undergoing of salvation and perfection does not detract from the excellence of the patient.

The Franciscan Gonsalvo

Question 4

Does Motion without a Terminus[1] *Imply a Contradiction?*

It seems that it does not, for there is motion without a terminus, for example the movement of the heavens.

On the contrary, the terminus of motion is identical with motion. So if you deny a terminus of motion you deny motion itself.

I reply that this does imply a contradiction, for nothing can be in motion unless it has been in motion before.[2] Furthermore, there would be potentiality without actuality.

Regarding the argument about the movement of the heavens, we are setting aside the question of the *terminus a quo* of the heavens' movement, so we have only to inquire about the *terminus in quo* and *ad quem* of motion.

The terminus in which *(in quo)* motion exists is the subject of motion, and this is the first mobile body.[3] The first mobile body is thus the first body, and because it is the first body it has less potentiality and consequently less motion; as the first mobile body it has the least motion. Some properties denote a perfection, others an imperfection. To be set in motion denotes an

1 As Eckhart explains, he uses *terminus* in three senses: *terminus a quo* (the starting point), *terminus in quo* (subject in which the motion exists), and *terminus ad quem* (purpose of the motion).

2 See Aristotle, *Physics*, VI, 6, 236b 33 ff; *Metaph.*, IX, 14, 1049b 35.

3 The *primum mobile*, or outermost sphere of the heavens, according to the astronomy of Ptolemy.

imperfection. Accordingly, the more perfect something is, the less it participates in motion and place; and because the heavenly body is in the first rank of perfection it is least subject to motion and place. It moves all things and determines their place. The earth determines nothing in place, water determines more, and going upward in this way [the heavenly body] has the least motion, for it moves only in place. Similarly it has only one place: it [moves] from one place to another only according to our way of thinking.[4]

Moreover, it is only one motion, and it is moved through its parts and not in its center; for it is the first mobile body, movable by the immobile [power] existing in it, because this denotes a perfection. So it should be moved in itself and not in its center.

The objection may be raised that parts have potential existence. I reply that the argument proves the opposite. Because they have potential existence [the first mobile body] is moved through them, for motion is the actuality of a being in potentiality.[5] The cause of mutability, and also of immutability, in all things is whole and part: whatever has existence fully is immutable, for example God. But whatever has only a part of existence is mutable. This is what Thomas says in his ***Questions On Evil***, in the article on demons, question two, in the solution of an argument.[6]

So the heavenly sphere is moved through its parts, because it is the first [mobile body]. As a result it has only one uniform movement, and thus it has no contrary. Astronomers have found

4 See Aristotle, *Physics*, VI, 9, 240a29-b9. St. Thomas, *In IV Phys.*, lect. 11 (Rome, 1894), 2, p. 315, n. 12; *In VIII Phys.*, lect. 23, p. 457, n. 6.

5 See Aristotle, *Physics*, III, 1, 201a 10.

6 St. Thomas, *De Malo*, 16, 2, ad 6.

diversity of movements in the sphere of the stars, so they claimed that it is not the first mobile body.[7]

In former times the *terminus ad quem* of the motion of the heavens was said to be the coming into being and passing away of sublunar bodies. But I, for my part, say that the heavens in their movement strive for the same end as matter. Now matter does not have a complete existence but only a partial one, with the result that it desires all forms. Because the heavenly sphere has quantity it has parts, and because it does not have a place it strives to acquire one. It moves in order that it might have the place of all parts, both right and left.

It can also be said that the body of the heavens is the loftiest of all. Now what is by nature higher influences and gives existence, while the lower by nature strives for existence. By nature the higher being is present to everything inferior, through itself as a whole and through each of its parts, to the inferior as a whole and to each of its parts. Since this cannot be done simultaneously, the superior exercises its influence on the inferior over a period of time.

What, then, is the terminus [of the movement of the heavens]? I answer that it does not strive for anything for itself, as neither does the eye see for itself but for the whole [body]. It exists for the whole [universe] and it serves this end through its whole being. Thus the end sought by the heavens in their movement is the existence of the universe, or the conservation of the universe.

7 See St. Thomas, *In XII Metaph.*, lect. 12; ed. R. Cathala (Turin, 1935), n. 2558.

Question 5

Did the Forms of the Elements Remain in the Body of Christ while Dying on the Cross?

Argument for the affirmative: When the primary [elements of a thing] are destroyed nothing else can remain. But here [in the body of Christ] certain qualities appear; consequently [the primary elements] remain.

On the contrary: Then there would be four distinct bodies [in the body of Christ].

First I raise the question here whether there are several substantial forms in every mixed body. My answer is that in each mixed body there is only one substantial form. Second, I shall explain how elements remain in a mixed body. Third, I shall show that no form remains in a dead body; that if it does remain it does not denote [the dead body], and if it does denote it this is only in a privative sense [i.e. 'corpse']; and that if one did remain in Christ it could not be said to be 'assumed'.

Regarding these matters I show 1) that the case is different with the destruction of the elements and of mixed bodies; 2) that existence belongs to the whole and not to a part; 3) that there is one simple existence of each whole; 4) that every effect is present in its cause and every inferior being in its superior, and that it exists in no other way and in no other place.

1. Concerning the first point, I say that among simple bodies air is destroyed and fire is produced. Universal Nature, which is like the father of a family,[1] intends this passing away, otherwise

1 See Aristotle, *De Generatione Animalium*, II, 4, 744b 16. For the notion of universal nature governing the universe, see Avicenna, *Metaph.*, VI, 5 (Venice, 1508), fol. 93v.

there could be no coming into being, nor could it provide for the universe. But Nature does not intend destruction for its own sake but only incidentally. Everything incidental is reducible to what is essential, and it is reduced by being reduced to a common genus. It [i.e. fire] is reduced to a species through the destruction of the form of air. In its material existence it is reducible to matter.

In mixed bodies the case is entirely different. When a mixed body is destroyed, other forms take the place [of the previous form]. Nature, looking after the good of the universe, intends the generation of everything and destruction in order to assist generation. Its first intention is the preservation of the universe, and only for its sake does it desire the privation [of anything]. Afterward [intermediate] forms are intended incidentally because of the aforesaid privation. As a consequence these intermediate forms are neither in a genus nor in a species, for they are reducible [to the original form] through the [aforesaid] privation. Hence a form of this kind posits no being but rather a privation, and nature does not intend this. Thus the privation [of form] which occurs at death is reducible to the living being.[2]

2. Second, I affirm that existence belongs to the whole and only to the whole.[3] And because the whole is one, so also is existence one. And since the part, as a part, is always one of many, the part is the basis of number, whereas the whole is grounded in unity and unity in the whole. So the part does not have existence, for there are many parts, and all are one, for existence is one. Hence the part as such has no existence; but it has existence only through the relation it bears to the whole as to existence. The part, lacking the whole, is non-being, but as

2 See St. Thomas, *In I De Gen. et Corr.*, lect. 8, (Rome, 1896), 3, p. 292, n. 3.
3 See below, p. 100.

related to the whole it has existence. As becoming has existence because it is ordained to existence, so a part is a way to the whole and to existence. Neither does an accident exist except through the whole, which is the nature of the first. There are ten primary genera, all receiving existence from the first.[4] For every part receives existence from the whole, in the whole, and in relation to the whole, because all things are through it and in it and related to it:[5] in it and through it are all things.[6]

3. Regarding the third point, I say that unity and the greatest simplicity belong to the whole, and this is existence, for existence is primary. It follows that existence must be one.

Moreover, parts do not bring existence with them; rather they receive existence. So there is only one existence; for unity is grounded in existence. Boethius says, "All things strive for existence."[7] Number, for instance, is nothing, for it is not one. Falling short of unity, number also falls short of existence. Because time is also number it is nothing; it is not one but number. Thus being and unity are convertible terms. As Boethius says, "Everything that is, is because it is one in number."[8]

4. Regarding the fourth point, I say that every effect exists in its cause and there alone. Polycletus is not the cause of a house as a man — that is accidental — , nor as Polycletus, nor as a housebuilder; but because he is actually building a house is he the cause of the house and of its being built.[9] Its being built comes to an end at once when the housebuilding stops, its being

4 The first in any genus or order must be some whole; among the ten primary genera substance is the first.

5 Coloss., I, 16.

6 Romans 11, 36.

7 Boethius, *De Consolatione Philosophiae*, III, pr. 11; CSEL 67, p. 72, lines 3-6.

8 Boethius, *In Isagogen Porphyrii Commenta* (ed. sec.), I, c. 10; CSEL 48, p. 162, line 2.

9 See Aristotle, *Physics*, II, 3, 195a 34-b 6; *Metaph.*, V, 2, 1013b 35-1014a 10.

built having for its ground the act of building. So it exists in this and from this and through this.

In this way in every superior being there exists [every inferior] as such; and insofar as the former exists, to that extent does the latter.[10] So there must be an order in nature, which consists in nothing else than the relation of superior to inferior. Water, for example, moves downward and upward through the motion of the moon, and that motion is swifter and more delightful. Another example is the sun.

Turning now to the first article, I assert:

1. There is only one substantial form in one composite, for a form gives existence and it is not an accident; and everything receives existence from that substantial form.

Again, existence is one. Now substantial form gives existence. Therefore it is one.

Again, form is substantial. Hence it confers existence through substance. Consequently it is one. Matter, however, is bare unless something is added to it.

Again, art presupposes alteration and so on, whereas generation directly concerns existence.

Again, every substantial form is totally in the whole and totally in every part, for it precedes every accidental form; and from this everything has its existence.

Again, matter and form are two principles, but they are one in their coming to be and in their existence. As they constitute one existence, they are not two. An example: the Father and Son breathe forth [the Holy Spirit as one principle].

2. Regarding the elements, I say that according to Avicenna in his *Sufficientia* I, 10, they remain in the substantial forms [of

10 See Eckhart's *Defense*, G. Théry, *op. cit.*, I, p. 230, n. 27.

the mixed bodies].[11] The Commentator, at the end of his exposition of the *De Caelo et Mundo*[12] and *Physics* I,[13] holds that the forms of the elements are subject to intension and remission owing to their closeness to matter. But Thomas teaches that the form of a mixed body has its own quality, which is a disposition for the form.[14] This form itself is present beforehand, and it is one single form. For example, the intellectual form [of man], being the most perfect of all forms, is at the same time sensitive; and the case is the same with other forms. Because it denotes a whole it is not something divided. And it virtually contains the whole in itself, and it is more united and profound. So much for the form of a mixed body.

3. That form [presumed to be in the dead body] of Christ, granted that it was present, does not denote [him], for it is in the process of becoming; in fact it is an accidental [form]. And if it does denote him, it does so only in a privative sense: pallid color, for example, does not denote anything positive. Also, granted that the form was present, it is not assumed [by the divine person],[15] for the personal existence [of Christ] always remained, and [the presumed] form is posterior to that existence.

11 Avicenna, *Sufficientia*, I, c. 10 (Venice, 1508), fol. 19.

12 Averroes, *In IV De Caelo et Mundo*, c. 40 (Venice, 1574), 5, fol. 267v-268r.

13 This doctrine has not been found in Averroes' commentary on the *Physics*.

14 St. Thomas, *De Mixtione Elementorum*, ed. J. Perrier, *Opuscula Omnia* (Paris, 1949), p. 22, n. 5. *Summa Theol.* I, 76, 4, ad 4.

15 That is, the intermediate form would not be united hypostatically to the divine person. See above, Introduction, p. 28.

II

PROLOGUES TO THE *OPUS TRIPARTITUM*

Summary of the Prologues

Notice that five chapters have been placed between the introductory General Prologue of the *Opus Tripartitum* and the *Commentary on Genesis*.

In chapter one, which comes first and begins "In order to clarify," there are two main points to observe. The first is that we should speak and think differently of general terms like being, unity, truth, goodness and others of this sort, which are convertible with being, and other terms that are below them and restricted to a genus, species or nature of being. The second is that inferior terms contribute absolutely nothing to superior terms, nor do they affect them, but conversely superior terms influence and affect their inferior terms.

In chapter two, which begins "Existence is God," you have the proposition that existence is God proved by five arguments.

In chapter four, which begins "In the beginning God created heaven and earth," you should notice four points in the explanation of the text. 1) God, and he alone, created heaven and earth and all things; the act of creation can be communicated to no one besides God. 2) He created all things in such a way that they are not outside himself, as ignorant people falsely imagine. Everything that God creates or does he does or creates in himself, sees or knows in himself, loves in himself. Outside himself he does nothing, knows or loves nothing; and this is peculiar to God himself. 3) God so created all things that he nevertheless always creates in the present. The act of creation does not fade into the past but is always in the beginning and in process and new. Similarly the Son has always been born in God, is always being born, as is said in Zechariah 6: "Here is a man whose name is 'Arising'," [1] — taking 'Arising' as a participle. Luke I says, "The Arising from on high has visited us." [2] 4) As soon as any action of God is done in its beginning, it is immediately perfect, as Deuteronomy 32 says: "The works of God are perfect."[3]

In chapter five, which begins "Existence is God," you have two points to notice in particular. 1) Being signifies nothing but existence, as "white [signifies] the quality alone," as the Philosopher says.[4] Similarly one signifies nothing but unity, true nothing but truth, good nothing but goodness. 2) We should speak and judge differently of being and this being, and similarly of one and this one, of true and this true, good and this good. When something is called being, one, true, good, each of these is a predicate of a proposition, and it lies second to the subject.[5] But when something is called this being, this one, this true, or this good (for example, a man or a stone or the like), then the 'this' and 'this' are the predicate of the proposition, and the general terms just mentioned (for example 'being') are not

1 Zechariah 6, 12.

2 Luke 1, 78.

3 Deuteronomy 32, 4.

4 Aristotle, *Categories*, 5, 3b 19. See St. Thomas: "Ens autem non dicit quidditatem, sed solum actum essendi, cum sit principium ipsum." *In I Sent.*, d. 8, q. 4, a. 2; ed. Mandonnet (Paris, 1929) I, p. 223.

5 *secundum adiacens*. For the distinction between propositions in which the verb 'is' serves as a predicate (*secundum adiacens*) and those in which it serves as a copula (*tertium adiacens*), see St. Thomas, *In II Perihermenias*, lect. 2 (Rome, 1882) I, pp. 79-80, nn. 2-5. See Aristotle, *Perihermenias*, 10, 19b 18-20.

predicates, nor do they lie second to the subject, but they connect the predicate with the subject. For instance, when I say "This is a man or stone," I do not predicate existence but I predicate man or stone or something of the kind. That is why it is true that Martin is a man even if no man exists. I am not saying that a man exists, nor do I predicate existence or the existence of the terms, but only their connection. When I say "A rose is red," I do not assert or affirm that a rose exists, nor that redness exists, but only the natural connection of the terms. So 'existence' or 'is' is not a subject or predicate but a third term besides them: it is the copula of the predicate with the subject.

Four conclusions follow from these two premises, especially from the second. 1) God alone properly speaking exists and is called being, one, true, and good. 2) Everything that is being, one, true, or good does not have this from itself but from God and from him alone. 3) From God himself each and every thing immediately is, is one, is true, and is good. 4) When something is said to be this existence or being, this one, this true, this good, the 'this' and 'this' add or confer absolutely nothing of entity, unity, truth or goodness to being, one, true, and good. In saying this I am not destroying the existence of things or taking their existence away; rather I am establishing it.

General Prologue

This general introductory prologue first states the author's intention, second the division of the work, third the order and manner of proceeding in it. Each of the three books will have its own special introductory prologue.

In this *Opus Tripartitum* the author intends to satisfy as best he can the wishes of certain zealous brethren who a long time ago persistently urged him and constantly pressed him to put down in writing the topics they were accustomed to hear from him in lectures and other school exercises, in sermons, and in daily discussions. These concern three matters in particular: 1) certain general, pithy statements, 2) novel, brief, and easy explanations of various questions, 3) unusual commentaries on many texts of both Testaments of Sacred Scripture, especially in those matters which they do not recall having read or heard elsewhere. They urged me to do this particularly because novel and unusual topics are a more pleasant stimulant to the mind than ordinary ones, though the latter may be more valuable and important.

So the whole Work itself is divided into three main parts: 1) the Book of General Propositions, 2) the Book of Questions, and 3) the Book of Commentaries.

The first Book, which contains a thousand propositions or more, is divided into fourteen treatises corresponding to the number of terms of which the propositions are formed. And because "opposites stand out more clearly if they are placed next to each other,"[6] and "opposites are the object of one and the same knowledge,"[7] each of these treatises is divided into two parts. In the first I state propositions about the term itself, and in the second, propositions about the opposite of the same term.

The first treatise is about existence and being and its opposite, which is nothing.

The second, about unity and the one and its opposite, which is many.

The third, about truth and the true and its opposite, which is false.

6 Aristotle, *De Caelo*, II, 6, 289a 7.

7 Aristotle, *Prior Analytics*, I, 1, 24a 21; *Topics*, I, 14, 105b 5.

The fourth, about goodness and the good and its opposite, evil.

The fifth, about love and charity and its opposite, sin.

The sixth, about the noble, virtuous, and right, and their opposites, the base, vicious, and wrong.

The seventh, about the whole and its opposite, part.

The eighth, about the common and indistinct and their opposites, the proper and distinct.

The ninth, about the nature of the superior and its opposite, the inferior.

The tenth, about the first and the last.

The leleventh, about idea and reason and their opposites, the unformed and privation.

The twelfth, about the expression 'by which it is' and the contrasting 'that which is'.

The thirteenth is about God himself, the highest existence, who "has no contrary except non-existence," as Augustine says.[8]

The fourteenth, about substance and accident.

The second Book, of Questions, is divided on the basis of the subject of the questions. I shall consider them in the order they have in the *Summa* of the illustrious and venerable friar Thomas of Aquino, though I do not treat of all of them but only a few, as the occasion arose for disputing, lecturing, and giving conferences.

The third Book, of Commentaries, is divided into two parts. The author treated and expounded certain texts of both Testaments more fully, especially in sermons, so it seemed

8 St. Augustine, *De Immortalitate Animae*, 12; PL 32, 1031; *De Moribus Ecclesiae et de Moribus Manichaeorum*, II, 1; PL 32, 1345.

proper to him to comment on them separately, and to call this the Book of Sermons. The Book of Commentaries is subdivided according to the number and order of the books of the Old and New Testaments whose texts are expounded in it.

All this would seem to require an ocean of words, but two factors lend to brevity, as far as this is possible, and tighten up the work: first, because the explanations here are very seldom found elsewhere, and some topics scarcely at all; second, because in the Book of Questions and Book of Commentaries I treat piecemeal and concisely only a very few matters. This is St. Augustine's procedure in the *Seven Books of Questions on the First Seven Books of the Old Testament*, and in his *Treatise on Eighty Three Questions*, his *Letter to Orosius*, and some other works of his.[9]

It should be noted that at first sight some items from the following propositions, questions, and commentaries will appear strange, doubtful or false. But they will be judged otherwise if they are examined in a more learned and intelligent way. What I have said will be found to be clearly confirmed by the truth and authority of Sacred Scripture itself, or of some of the saints and illustrious masters.

In order to clarify what follows three preliminary points should be made.

1. We should by no means imagine or think of universal terms like existence, unity, truth and wisdom, godness, and so on, after the manner and nature of accidents. Accidents receive existence in and through their subject and through its change.

9 St. Augustine, *Quaestionum in Heptateuchum Libri VII*; CCL 33, 1-377; *De Diversis Quaestionibus Octoginta Tribus*; PL 40, 11-100; *Ad Orosium contra Priscillianistas et Origenistas*; PL 42, 669-678.

Moreover, they are posterior to the subject and take on existence by inhering in it, so that they are numbered and divided in it, so much so that the subject is placed in the definition of this sort of accidents, in as much as they have existence in it. The case is completely different with the general terms mentioned above. Existence itself, and the terms convertibly the same as it, are not added to things as though posterior to them; on the contrary they are prior to every aspect of things. It is not the nature of existence itself to be in something or from something or through something; neither is it added or joined to anything. On the contrary, it precedes and comes before everything. So the existence of everything is immediately from the first and universal cause of all things. All things exist from existence itself, and through it and in it, while existence is not in something or from something; for what is different from existence is not or is nothing. Existence itself is related to everything as its actuality and perfection; it is the actuality of all things, even of forms.[10] For this reason Avicenna says in his *Metaphysics* VIII, 6: "What everything desires is existence and the perfection of existence, inasmuch as it is existence." And he adds, "Therefore what is truly desired is existence."[11]

This is why the metaphysician investigates everything, even though it is mobile and changeable, insofar as it is being, even matter itself, the root of corruptible things. Furthermore, the existence of all things, insofar as it is existence, is by no means measured by time but by eternity. The intellect (whose object is being, and in which being comes before all else, according to Avicenna)[12] abstracts from here and now and consequently from

10 See St. Thomas, *Summa Theol.* I, 4, 1, ad 3.

11 Avicenna, *Metaph.* VIII, 6 A (Venice, 1508), fol. 100ra.

12 *Ibid.*, I, 6; fol. 72rb.

time. Augustine alludes to this in his book *On the Trinity* VII, 1, when he says, "Wisdom is wise, and it is wise by itself. Every soul becomes wise by participating in wisdom; and if it again becomes foolish, still wisdom remains in itself, nor does it undergo a change when the soul has been changed into folly. It is not in man, who is made wise by it, as whiteness is in the body, which is made white by it; for when the body was changed into another color that whiteness will not remain but will cease to be at all."[13]

2. It should be noted well in advance that it is always the case that the prior and superior takes absolutely nothing from the posterior, nor is it affected by anything in it. On the contrary, the prior and superior influences the inferior and posterior and descends into it with its own properties and assimilates it to itself, as a cause influences an effect and an agent a patient. It is the nature of the first and superior, being "rich in itself,"[14] to influence and affect the inferior with its properties, among which are unity and indivision. What is divided in the inferior is always one and undivided in the superior. It clearly follows that the superior is in no way divided in the inferior; but, while remaining undivided, it gathers together and unites what is divided in the inferior. An obvious example of this is the parts of animals. The soul is not divided in them, but while remaining undivided it unites the individual parts in itself, so that they have one soul, one life, one existence, and one living. So true is this that if we were to imagine a man's head at the north pole and his feet at the south pole, his foot will not be farther from his head than from itself, nor will it be below the head, as far as

13 St. Augustine, *De Trinitate*, VII, 1, 2; CCL 50, xvi, 1 (Turnholt, 1968), p. 248, lines 137-144.

14 The expression is from the *Liber de Causis*; see below, note 72.

existence, living, soul, and life are concerned. In unity there is no distance, nothing below the other, absolutely no distinction of shape, degree or actuality.

3. Finally, it should be noted beforehand that the second Book, and so too the third, are so dependent on the first, namely the Book of Propositions, that without it they are of little use, because the explanations of questions and the commentaries on [Scriptural] texts are usually based on one of the propositions. So that you might see this by an example and know the manner of proceeding in the whole *Opus Tripartitum*, I shall give a preliminary statement of the first proposition, the first question, and the first commentary on a text.

The first proposition is "Existence is God." The first question concerning the divinity is "Does God exist?" The first text of Sacred Scripture is "In the beginning God created heaven and earth."[15] Let us first see how the proposition is explained, second how the question is solved by it, and third how this text is elucidated by the same proposition.

Existence is God

This proposition is evident:

1. First, because if existence is something different from God himself, God neither exists nor is he God. How can that be, or be something from which existence is different and distinct, or to which it is foreign? Or if God exists, in that case he exists by another, since existence is different from him. Therefore God and existence are identical, or God has existence from another, and then he is not God himself, as was said above, but something else is before him and is the cause of his existence.

15 Genesis 1, 1.

2. Moreover, everything that exists has the fact that it may be or is through and by existence. Therefore, if existence is different from God, a thing has existence from something other than God.

3. Moreover, before existence there is nothing. Hence whatever confers existence creates, and is the creator; creation indeed is the giving of existence from nothing. Now plainly everything has existence from existence itself, as everything is white by whiteness. Consequently, if existence were different from God, the creator would be other than God.

4. Again, everything having existence exists in the absence of everything else, just as that which has whiteness is white. Therefore, if existence is different from God, things will be able to exist without God, and then God is not the first cause nor the cause of the existence of things.

5. Besides, outside of existence and before existence there is only nothing. Hence, if existence were different from God and foreign to him, God would be nothing, or, as was said before, he would exist by something other than himself and before himself, and that would be God to God himself, and the God of all things. This is suggested by the text of Exodus, "I am who am."[16]

The First Question Is: Does God Exist?

I reply that he does. This follows from the proposition just elucidated.

1. If God does not exist, nothing exists. The consequent is false and therefore the antecedent is also false, namely that God does not exist. The inference is proved as follows: If existence

16 Exodus 3, 14.

does not exist, no being exists, or nothing exists, as nothing white exists if whiteness does not exist. Now existence is God, as the proposition states. Hence, if God does not exist, nothing exists. The falsity of the conclusion is proved by nature, the senses, and reason.

2. A second argument can be given for our main thesis. There is no truer proposition than one in which the same thing is predicated of itself, for example that man is man. Now existence is God. Therefore it is true that God exists.

3. Nothing can be separated from itself, as Augustine says in his book *On the Immortality of the Soul.*[17] But, as was said before, existence is God. Therefore existence cannot be separated from God so that he does not exist.

4. A thing is what it is through nothing other than itself, as Avicenna says.[18] Thus, whether any man actually exists or not, man is a rational, mortal animal. Augustine states that nothing is so eternal as the nature of a circle.[19] Now existence is the essence of God, or God himself. Consequently it is an eternal truth that God exists. It follows that he exists. The conclusion is evident, for everything that exists, exists through existence, and existence is God. This is what is written in Exodus 3: "He who is sent me."[20]

"In the beginning God created heaven and earth" [21]

Notice that there are four points in the elucidation of the first text through the above proposition — points that will also be

17 St. Augustine, *De Immortalitate Animae*, 8; PL 32, 1028.
18 Avicenna, *Metaph*. V, 1; fol. 86va-87rb; I, 6, fol. 71rb-72ra.
19 St. Augustine, *De Immortalitate Animae*, 4; PL 32, 1024.
20 Exodus 3, 14.
21 Genesis 1, 1.

used in expounding other texts. This will be my procedure in the whole Book of Commentaries and Sermons: in explaining one text I shall briefly and incidentally clarify many others, each of which must be expounded according to plan and at greater length in its proper place.

I say then that through the proposition elucidated above it is proved 1) that God, and he alone, created heaven and earth (in other words, the heights and the depths), and consequently all things; 2) that he created in the beginning, that is, in himself; 3) that he indeed created in the past, but nevertheless he is always in the beginning of creation and begins to create; 4) that creation and every work of God is at once perfect and finished in the very beginning of creation; for the text says, "In the beginning he *created*" which is a verb of the perfect tense.[22]

The first of these four points is evident as follows: Creation is the giving of existence. We do not have to add "from nothing," because before existence there is nothing. Now it is certain that existence is given to things by existence and by it alone. It follows that God, and he alone, creates or has created, because he is existence. This also clearly solves the problem whether the act of creation can be shared by anything else; but this will be more fully apparent in its appropriate place.[23]

The second of the four points, that he created in the beginning, that is, in himself, can be shown as follows: Creation gives or confers existence. Now existence is the beginning and first of

22 *verbum praeteriti perfecti temporis*. According to Priscian, this tense is used if a present action has been started and brought to conclusion: "Si enim ad finem perveniat praesens inceptum, statim utimur praeterito perfecto." Priscian, *Institutiones Grammaticae*, VIII, 53; ed. M. Hertz (Leipzig, 1860), I, p. 415, lines 16-17.

23 See *Comm. in Sap.*, ed. G. Théry, *Archives d'histoire doctrinale et littéraire du moyen âge*, 4 (1929), p. 281, lines 3-6; German sermon 82, ed. F. Pfeiffer, *Meister Eckhart*, p. 263, lines 6-8.

all things; before it and outside of it there is nothing; and this is God. So he created all things in the beginning, that is in himself. For he created everything in existence, which is the beginning, and this is God himself. Here it should be noticed that everything God creates, works or does, he works or does in himself. What is outside of God, and is made outside of him, exists and is made outside of existence; but in fact it is not made, because being made ends in existence. Augustine says in his *Confessions* IV: God made all things: "He did not make them and then depart, but they are from him and in him."[24]

It is different with other craftsmen. The builder of a house builds a house outside of himself, both because there are other things outside of him, and because wood and stones, in which the house exists and out of which it is made, do not have existence from the builder or in him but from another and in another. So we should not falsely imagine that God has, as it were, hurled or created creatures outside of himself in some infinite space or void; for nothing receives nothing, nor can it be the subject or term or end of any action. If something is said to be received in nothing, or to be terminated in nothing, it is not a being but nothing. So God created all things not like other craftsmen, so that they stand outside of himself, or beside himself, or apart from himself. Rather, he called them out of nothingness, that is from non-existence, to existence, so that they might find and receive and have it in him; for he himself is existence. That is why the text aptly says that God created not *from* the beginning but *in* the beginning. How would they exist if not in existence, which is the beginning? Along the same lines I explain below the text of Wisdom 1: "God created, so that all

24 St. Augustine, *Confessions*, IV, 12; CSEL 33 (Vienna, 1896), p. 78, line 16.

things might have being,"[25] and Romans 4: "He calls things that are not yet in existence [as if they already were],"[26] and several other similar statements.

Another point to observe is that just as something can be accidental to that which exists, but nothing can be accidental to existence itself, as Boethius says,[27] so something can be outside of everything that exists, but nothing can be outside of existence itself.

The third of the four points, that God created in the past, and yet he is always in the beginning of creation and begins to create, is explained as follows: God, as existence, acts in existence and toward existence. Wisdom 1: "He created, so that all things might have being."[28] Now existence is the beginning, the first, and the source of all things. From this it is clear that every work of God is new. Wisdom 7: "Remaining in himself, he makes all things new."[29] Apocalypse 22: "Behold, I make all things new."[30] So it is said in Isaiah: "I am the first and the last."[31] He so created, therefore, that he nevertheless always creates; for what is in the beginning, and whose end is the beginning, always arises, always is being born, always has been born. Augustine says in his *Confessions* I: "All the things of yesterday and times past, you will do today, you have done today." [32] Therefore he created everything in the beginning,

25 Wisdom 1, 14.

26 Romans 4, 17.

27 Boethius, *Quomodo Substantiae Bonae Sint (De Hebdomadibus)*; PL 64, 1311 BC. *Boethius. The Theological Tractates*, ed. H. F. Stewart and E. K. Rand (London, 1953), p. 40, lines 35-40.

28 Wisdom 1, 14.

29 Wisdom 2, 27.

30 Apocalypse 21, 5.

31 Isaiah 44, 6.

32 St. Augustine, *Confessions*, I, 6; CSEL 33, p. 8, lines 18-20.

because in himself who is the beginning. And again, he created in himself, the beginning, because things past and gone he creates today, as it were in the beginning and in the first instant. Neither of these is true of other workmen: they do not work within themselves, and they leave their works because they stop working.

The fourth and final point, that creation and every work of God is at once perfect and finished in the very beginning of creation, is obvious from what has been said. When the end and beginning coincide, something necessarily is at once made and has been made, at once begins and is completed. Now God, as existence, is the commencement, beginning, and end. For just as there is nothing before existence, so there is nothing after it, because all becoming ends in existence. What exists as such is neither made nor can be made. Hence "When 'states' are present, movement stops."[33] What is a house is not made to be a house, though it can be made white or something of the sort, but only insofar as it is not white. Thus creation, and every work of God, is perfect as soon as it begins. As Deuteronomy 32 says, "The works of God are perfect;"[34] and the Psalm, "He spoke and they were made." [35] For he is the commencement or "beginning and end," as is said in the first and last chapters of the Apocalypse.[36]

Let us briefly summarize each point as follows:

1. Existence is the very essence of God. So all things receive existence from him and from him alone. Therefore God created heaven and earth. So much for the first point.

33 Aristotle, *De Generatione et Corruptione*, I, 7, 324b 17.

34 Deuteronomy 32, 4.

35 Psalm 148, 5.

36 Apocalypse 1, 8; 22, 13.

2. Again, outside of God, that is, outside of existence, there is nothing. Consequently either he did not create or he created everything in himself, who is the beginning. So much for the second. As Augustine says, "They are from him and in him."[37]

3. God, as existence, is the first and the last, the beginning and the end. Therefore everything that he created past he creates as present in the beginning, and what he creates or does now as in the beginning he created at the same time in the completed past. Augustine says, "All the things of yesterday you will do today, you have done today."[38] So much for the third and fourth points.

And because here the end is the beginning, the completed is always starting and the born is always being born. This is how God created all things: he does not stop creating, but he forever creates and begins to create. As we read in John 5: "My father works up to now, and I work."[39] Augustine says, "He did not create and then leave," and so on.[40] For creatures are always in the process and beginning of their creation. This is what Scripture says: "In the beginning God created heaven and earth."[41] He begins with that with which he finishes and ends, for the end is the beginning; and he ends or finishes with that with which he begins, because the commencement is the end. (Apocalypse, first and last chapters).[42]

Finally, notice that all, or almost all, the questions concerning God are easily solved through the first proposition stated above,

37 St. Augustine, *Confessions*, IV, 12; CSEL 33, p. 78, line 16.

38 *Ibid.*, I, 6, p. 8, lines 18-20. See Eckhart, *The Book of Divine Comfort*, 3; transl. Blakney, p. 72.

39 John 5, 17.

40 St. Augustine, *Confessions*, IV, 12; CSEL 33, p. 78, line 16.

41 Genesis 1, 1.

42 See Apocalypse 1, 8; 22, 13.

if the inference is well made; and most of what is written about him, even obscure and difficult matters, are clearly explained by natural reason.

I have now explained the three preceding topics: the proposition, the question, and the [Scriptural] text, in a brief and introductory way. They will be treated more fully in their proper places, at the beginning of the three Books.

The Book of Propositions

Prologue

Existence is God. Here begins the first part of the *Opus Tripartitum*, namely the Book of Propositions, whose first treatise concerns existence and being and its opposite, nothing.

In order to elucidate the matter of this treatise and several others to follow, certain matters should be noted by way of introduction.

The first is that just as "white signifies only the quality [of whiteness]," as the Philosopher says, so being signifies only existence.[43] The same is also true in other cases; for example, one signifies nothing but unity, true truth, good goodness, noble nobility, right rectitude, just justice, and so on with other terms and their opposites: evil for instance signifies only malice, false nothing but falsity, wrong wrongness, unjust injustice, and so on.

Second, it should be observed that we must think differently about being and about this or that being, and similarly about existence absolutely and purely and simply, with no addition,

43 See above, note 4.

and about existence of this or that sort. The same is true of other terms, for example of the good absolutely and this or that good, or of the good of this and the good for that. For when I say that something exists, or I predicate one, true or good, these four terms feature in the predicate as the second term [of the proposition], and they are used formally and substantively. But when I say that something is *this*, for instance a stone, and that it is one stone, a true stone, or a good *this*, namely a stone, these four terms are used as the third term of the proposition.[44] They are not predicates but the copula, or they are 'placed near' the predicate.

So observe in a preliminary way: 1) God alone is properly being, one, true, and good. 2) From him all things are and are one, true, and good. 3) All things immediately owe to him the fact that they are and that they are one, true, and good. 4) When I say this being, or this one, or that one, this or that true, this or that good, 'this' or 'that' adds absolutely nothing, or makes no addition, of entity, unity, truth or goodness, to being, one, true, good.

The first of these four points, that God alone is properly being, is evident from Exodus 3: "I am who am"; "He who is sent me";[45] and from Job: "You who alone are."[46] And Damascene says that the first name of God is "The reality that is."[47] In support of this is the fact that Parmenides and Melissus, the first philosophers, held that there is only one being, but that there are many beings of this or that kind, for

44 *tertium adiacens propositionis*. See above, note 5.

45 Exodus 3, 14.

46 Job 14, 4.

47 *Quod est.* See St. John Damascene, *De Fide Orthodoxa*, I, 9; ed. E. M. Buytaert (St. Bonaventure, New York, 1955), p. 48, n. 2. This text of Damascene reads *qui est*; however, a variant reading is *quod est.*

example, fire, earth, and the like, as Avicenna explains in his *Physics*, which he calls *Sufficientia*.[48] Also confirming this is the text of Deuteronomy 6 and Galatians 3: "God is one."[49] So the truth of the above proposition "Existence is God" is now evident. This is why the one asking who or what God is, is given the reply: existence. As the text of Exodus 3, cited above, says: "I am who am," and "He who is."[50]

Again, the case is the same with the one: God alone in the proper sense is the One, or is one. As Deuteronomy 6 says, "God is one."[51] In support of this is the fact that Proclus and the *Book of Causes* often call God by the name One or Unity.[52] Moreover, 'one' is the negation of negation,[53] and hence it applies solely to the primary and complete existence, which is God, of whom nothing can be denied because he at once precontains and includes all existence.

The case is the same with the true. According to John 14, "I am the truth."[54] Augustine, in his book *On the Trinity*, VIII, 2, says "God is truth, because God is light." And further on: "When you hear that he is truth, do not ask, what is truth? Remain, therefore, if you can, in that first flash when you were dazzled as it were by its brightness, when it was said to you 'truth'."[55] Augustine means that this is God.

48 Avicenna, *Sufficientia*, I, 4; fol. 16ra-16va. See Aristotle, *Metaph.* I, 5, 986b 10-987a 2.

49 Deuteronomy 6, 4; Galatians 3, 20.

50 Exodus 3, 14. In a German sermon Eckhart says: "Under allen namen ist kein eigner danne der dâ ist." *Sermo Germ.* 30; ed. Pfeiffer, *Meister Eckhart*, p. 108, line 28.

51 Deuteronomy 6, 4.

52 Proclus, *Elements of Theology*, 1-6; 113-115; ed. E. R. Dodds, 2nd ed. (Oxford, 1963), pp. 2-7, 100-103. *Liber de Causis*, 9; ed. Bardenhewer (Freiburg im B., 1882), p. 174, lines 2-5.

53 For the 'negation of negation', see above p. 33.

54 John 14, 6.

55 St. Augustine, *De Trinitate*, VIII, 2; CCL, 50, p. 271, lines 30-35.

Once again, the case is the same with the good. Luke 18 says, "no one is good except God";[56] and Matthew 9, "No one is good save the one God."[57] Proclus says in proposition 12: "The principle and first cause of all beings is the good."[58] Supporting this is the fact that according to Dionysius the first name of God is the good,[59] and that Augustine says in his book *On the Trinity*, VIII, 3, "See the good itself, if you can; so you will see God, the good of every good."[60]

So much for the first of the four points: that God alone is in the proper sense being, one, true, and good. Every other thing is *this* being, for example, a stone, a lion, a man, and so on, and *this* one, *this* true, *this* good, for example, a good mind, a good angel, and so on.

The second of the four points, that all things have existence, one existence, true existence, good existence from God alone, is clear from what has been said. How indeed would anything exist except by existence and through existence, or be one except by one and through one or unity, or be true without truth, or good except through goodness, as, for instance, everything white is white by whiteness?

Moreover, Boethius in his *Consolation of Philosophy* teaches that as the good and the true are grounded and established through existence and in existence, so also existence is grounded and established in the one and through the one.[61] So just as all things have existence from God, who is existence, so also they

56 Luke 10, 8.
57 Mark 10, 18.
58 Proclus, *The Elements of Theology*, 12, p. 15.
59 Dionysius, *De Divinis Nominibus*, III, 1; PG 3, 680 B.
60 St. Augustine, *De Trinitate*, VIII, 3; CCL 50, p. 272, lines 15-17.
61 Boethius, *De Consolatione Philosophiae*, III, pr. 2; CSEL 67, pp. 47-49. See Proclus, *Elements of Theology*, 13; ed. Dodds, pp. 15-17.

have from him one existence, good existence, and similarly true existence. For these three [i.e. existence, unity, and goodness] are what they are in the truth and through the truth. That does not exist which does not truly exist, nor is that one which is not truly one, nor is that good which is not truly good. That is not gold which is not truly gold, and so on in all cases.

Again, being, one, true, and good are primary in things and are common to everything. So they are present to, and in, everything before the coming of any cause that is not the first and universal cause of all things; they are in [everything] solely from the first and universal cause of all things. Nevertheless this does not deprive secondary causes of their own influences. The form of fire does not give existence to the fire but *this* existence, nor one existence but *this* one existence; that is [it makes it to be] fire and one fire. The case is the same with the true and the good. But the very fact that the form of fire, for instance, causes the existence of one, true, good fire, has been determined by the first cause, as the ***Book of Causes*** says, "Every intelligence has its fixed character and essence through pure goodness, which is the first cause," and according to the commentary on this proposition.[62]

As was said above, moreover, nothing, or no existence, can be denied to being or of being; rather, the negation of negation is aptly ascribed to it.[63] So nothing one, or no unity, can be denied to one except the negation of negation of unity or one; and the case is the same with the true and good. This clearly shows that each and every being owes to God the fact that it exists, is one, is true, and is good. And every being not only possesses each of

62 *Liber de Causis*, 8; ed. Bardenhewer, p. 172, lines 2-3; the commentary follows the proposition.

63 See above, p. 95.

these from God himself, but it possesses them from him without any intermediary.

This is the third main point of the four stated above, namely that each and every being not only holds its entire existence, unity, truth, and goodness from God, but it does so directly, with absolutely no intermediary. How could something exist if an intermediary came between it and existence, and consequently stood outside of and, as it were, next to and beyond existence itself? Now existence is God. The case is the same with the one and every one, with the true and every true, with the good and every good. If any feature of a thing is not immediately touched by existence itself, nor formed by being permeated with it, it is nothing. Similarly if anything is not touched by the one, nor formed or clothed by being permeated with it, it is not one. And the case is the same with the true and the good. This is what the Book of Wisdom 8 says of wisdom, which is God: "It reaches from end to end mightily,"[64] and Isaiah says, "I am the first and the last."[65] The first does not admit of an intermediary. Thus it is said in the beginning of the *Book of Causes* that the influence of the first cause comes first and leaves last: it comes first because it is the first; it leaves last because it is the last.[66]

Furthermore, because God with his whole existence is absolutely one, or one being, he must be immediately present with his whole self to every whole, not to one part after another part, nor to a part through a part, as Augustine beautifully explains in his *Confessions* I.[67] This can be observed in the case of every

64 Wisdom 8, 1.
65 Isaiah 44, 6.
66 *Liber de Causis*, 1; ed. Bardenhewer, p. 163.
67 St. Augustine, *Confessions*, I, 3; CSEL 33, p. 3, lines 10-16.

substantial form. The soul with its whole self, without an intermediary, is immediately present to, and informs, the whole living body. Similarly without a mediator the form of fire at once invests and forms the whole essence of its matter by permeating it with its whole self, not one part after another, but each part with its whole self. This is why, according to *Metaphysics* VII, it is the whole, not its parts, that is produced and exists.[68] This is also why generation is instantaneous and not continuous, not a process but the end of a process. This clearly shows the mistake of those who place certain degrees, as it were formal intermediaries, between the essence of matter and the essential form of a mixed body.[69] If, therefore, every essential form with its whole self immediately clothes and informs the whole matter by permeating it essentially, this will be especially true of existence itself, which is universally and essentially the formal actuality of every form.[70]

The statement that each and every being immediately holds from God himself its whole existence, its whole unity, truth, and goodness, can also be explained as follows: No existence, or mode or difference of existence, can be wanting or lacking to existence itself. If anything were wanting or lacking to existence, it would not exist and it would be nothing. Now God is existence. And the same must be said of unity: what is wanting or lacking to unity is not one, nor does it produce what is one, nor can it be a mode or difference of unity. An equally valid argument can lead to the same conclusion regarding the true and the good.

68 Aristotle, *Metaph.* VII, 8, 1033b 17.

69 See above, Parisian Question 5, pp. 74-75. See William de la Mare, *Correctorium in primam partem*, art. 27 et 31; ed. Glorieux, *Le Correctorium Corruptorii "Quare"* (Kain, Belgium, 1927), pp. 115, 129-135.

70 See above, note 10.

Absolutely nothing of entity, then, can be denied to being or existence itself. It follows that nothing can be denied to the being itself which is God except the negation of negation of all existence. This is why unity, which is the negation of negation, is most closely related to being. And just as being is related to beings, so one is related to everything one in any way whatsoever or any difference of unity, and the true is related to everything true, and the good to each and every good thing. So this or that being, this or that one, this or that true, this or that good, insofar as it is this or that, adds or imparts absolutely nothing of entity, unity, truth, and goodness. This is the fourth main point made above.

In saying this I am not depriving things of existence or destroying their existence, but on the contrary I am establishing it. For the present I shall explain this in two ways, first by examples, second by arguments.

The examples are three in number: 1) matter and form, 2) parts and their whole, 3) the man assumed by the Word.

1. Matter clearly contributes no existence to the composite, nor by itself does it have absolutely any existence apart from that which the form confers on the composite. Nevertheless I do not say on this account that matter is nothing, but rather that it is a substance and the other part of the composite.

2. Individual parts contribute absolutely no existence to their whole; rather, they receive their total existence from their whole and in their whole. Otherwise the whole would not be one: it would be as many in number as the parts, if each part added its own existence to the whole. Now it is more impossible for two or more existences to be present, or to be intermingled, in one, than for several essential forms to be present in one subject; for existence is through itself and by itself the principle of distinction [between things]. Hence it is impossible that something

having several existences be one existence; and conversely, that something having several forms different in genus, for example, forms of all the categories, be one in number from the unity of existence of the whole composite, for example, of Peter or Martin.

3. I grant that in the man assumed by the Word there is the one personal hypostatic existence of the Word itself, and yet Christ was truly a man in exactly the same sense as other men. So in the present instance it is much more the case regarding a creature with respect to its creator than regarding matter with respect to form, and parts with respect to the whole, as God is a more intimate, primary, perfect, and universal cause.

My second main intent is to prove my statement by arguments.

1. Whatever gives existence creates and is the first and universal cause of all things, as was said above. Now nothing that is this or that is the first and universal cause of everything, nor does it create. Hence, nothing that is this or that gives existence. Augustine says this in his *Confessions* I: "There is no other vein by which being and life flows into us except this, that you, O Lord, have made us." And further on he adds, "What is it to me, if someone does not understand?"[71]

2. Moreover, "The First is rich by itself," as the twentieth proposition of the *Book of Causes* says.[72] Now it would not be rich by itself, nor the first, if something else besides itself gave existence. So nothing that is this or that being gives existence, though forms give this or that existence, insofar as it is this or that, but not insofar as it is existence. Thus, according to John

71 St. Augustine, *Confessions*, I, 6; CSEL 33, p. 8, lines 7-9.

72 *Liber de Causis*, 20; ed. Bardenhewer, p. 182, line 16.

1, "All things made by him are, and without him nothing is made";[73] for 'are' and 'is' mean existence.

3. From this I can argue for my position as follows: Outside of existence, and without existence, everything is nothing, even what has been made. Therefore, if something else besides God caused existence, God would not give existence to everything, nor would he influence anything, or what he gave or influenced would be nothing. This contradicts the text of James 1: "He gives to all men abundantly"[74] and Romans 11, "From him and through him and in him are all things,"[75] and similar texts.

4. This or that good, and this or that being, hold their entire existence from existence and through existence and in existence. Hence this or that does not in return impart any existence to existence itself, from which it receives existence as from a cause. Examples of this can be seen everywhere. A white shield receives its whole white existence, insofar as it is white, from whiteness; it has absolutely no whiteness from itself. And insofar as it is a shield it returns nothing to whiteness itself. In this connection it should be clearly noted that what makes a thing truly one is the fact that it has as a whole each of its elements through one single [principle]. For example, a mixed body as a whole is quantified by quantity alone: outside of quantity none of the elements in the body adds any quantity, neither matter nor form nor any quality, and so on. Again, the same body is as a whole qualified by quality alone; for example, a white body by whiteness, a black body by blackness, and so on. None of the other elements, neither matter, form, quantity, nor anything else of this sort, adds or gives or increases absolutely

73 John 1, 3.
74 James 1, 5.
75 Romans 11, 36.

any quality. Even more so a whole composite, like a stone, has the existence of a stone from the form of stone, but it has existence absolutely from God alone as from the first cause.

Again, we should not imagine that each cause of a thing — efficient, final, formal, and material — brings and gives existence to the composite separately, but that a thing as a whole, with all its parts and properties, holds the same existence totally from its end alone as from a final cause alone, from its form as from a formal cause, and from its matter passively or receptively.

Moreover, if one and the same thing has several causes of the same kind, for example several efficient or final causes, they do not constitute a mere number, but one is under the other, the lower being in the power of the higher, and by a single action they bring about the same numerical effect in the product. Two causes, insofar as they are two, produce different effects. It is especially important to realize this regarding all causes in relation to the first and highest cause, which is God.

What has been said can be briefly summarized in these seven points:

1. Being signifies nothing but existence, one nothing but unity, true nothing but truth, and good nothing but goodness.

2. Our language about being must be different from our language about this or that being, and also about other terms such as one, true, and good. Thus there is only one being, and this is God; but there are many beings that are this or that. The same holds for one, true, and good, as was said before.

3. The third point is the reason for the second. For when I call something being, one, true, or good, each of these is the predicate of a proposition and it is taken formally and substantively. But when I say something is this being, this one (for

example, a man), or this true, or this or that good, none of these is a predicate, but a copula or a term 'lying near' the predicate.

4. God alone in the proper sense is being, one, true, and good.

5. From God alone all things are, are one, true, and good.

6. All things immediately owe to God the fact that they are, that they are one, true, and good.

7. Nothing created brings or contributes to things any entity, unity, truth or goodness.

After setting forth these matters in order to clarify what is to follow, I shall now begin with the proposition: Existence is God, and so on.

II. Book of Questions

Prologue (missing)

III. Book of Commentaries

Prologue

This is the Prologue to the Book of Commentaries. It contains five noteworthy points.

1. When expounding a [Scriptural] text under discussion, many other texts [of Scripture] are often cited; and all these passages can be explained in their proper places by means of this one, just as at present it is explained by means of them.

2. All the texts cited and mentioned almost incidentally are always explained more fully in their proper places. He who wishes to understand them more fully should look there.

3. These passages are often cited [with a meaning] that goes beyond the primary meaning of the text, but they are to the

point, considering the true and proper sense of the words. Examples are: "A little while, and you will see me no more" (John 16);[76] "... a little leaven leavens all the dough" (1 Cor. 5),[77] and many other similar texts. Augustine teaches the utility and value of this procedure in his *Confessions* XII, when commenting on the text of Genesis 1: "In the beginning God created heaven and earth."[78]

4. So that the Book will not be unduly long, I shall often simply touch upon a distinction in the text and some noteworthy matters in it and arising from the text under discussion. It will be left to the experienced reader to delve further into Scripture and to harmonize it.

5. The main texts are often expounded in many ways, so that the reader may take now one explanation, now another, either one or several, as he thinks fit. For the sake of brevity I also consciously omit many matters worthy of note.

76 John 16, 16.

77 I Cor. 5, 6.

78 St. Augustine, *Confessions*, XII, 31; CSEL 33, p. 343, lines 1-17.

APPENDIX

Eckhart's Exegesis of the Divine Name 'I am who am' in his Commentary on the Book of Exodus[1]

"I am who am"[2]

There are four points to notice here. The first is that these three words 'I', 'am', 'who' most fittingly apply to God. 'I' is a first person pronoun. A discrete pronoun,[3] it signifies pure substance — pure, I say, without any accident, without anything alien, substance without quality,[4] without this or that form, without this or that. Now this properly describes God and him alone, who is above accident, above species, above genus: God alone, I say, and for this reason we read in the Psalm "I alone am."[5]

Again, 'who' is an indefinite word,[6] and what is indefinite and infinite is appropriate to God alone.

Further, 'am' is a substantive word.[7] Regarding 'word' see John 1, [1]: "The word was God"; regarding 'substantive' see Hebrews 1, [3]: "upholding all things by the word of his power."

The second point to notice is that when God says "I am," 'am' is here the predicate of the sentence and the second element

1 Eckhart's commentary on 'I am who am' has been translated by J. M. Clark and J. V. Skinner in *Meister Eckhart. Selected Treatises and Sermons* (London, 1958), pp. 225-230. It is translated here again because of its pertinence to the subject of this book. The Latin text is in *LW* II, pp. 20-31.

2 Exodus 3, 14.

3 See Priscian, *Instit. gram.*, XVII, c. 9, n. 56; ed. M. Hertz (Leipzig, 1860), II, p. 141, lines 17-19.

4 See *ibid.*, XII, c. 3, n. 15; I, p. 585, lines 32 ff.

5 Psalm 140, 10.

6 Priscian, *ibid.*, XIII, c. 6, n. 31; II, p. 20, lines 26-30.

7 *Ibid.*, VIII, c. 10, n. 51; I, p. 414, lines 13-16.

in the sentence.[8] Whenever this is the case, it signifies pure and naked existence in the subject and regarding the subject, and that it is the subject, in other words the essence of the subject, thus expressing the identity of essence and existence which is proper to God alone, whose quiddity is his *anitas*, as Avicenna says,[9] and who has no quiddity except *anitas* alone, which is expressed by existence.

The third point to notice is that the repetition of 'am' in the statement "I am who am" points out the purity of the affirmation, which excludes every negation from God. It also indicates a certain reversion and turning back of his being into and upon itself, and its abiding or remaining in itself; also a sort of boiling up or giving birth to itself: an inward glowing, melting and boiling in itself and into itself, light in light and into light wholly penetrating its whole self, totally and from every side turned and reflected upon itself. As the wise man says: "Monad begets — or begot — monad, and reflected its love or ardor upon itself."[10] This is why John 1 says: "In him was life."[11] Life means a sort of thrusting out, whereby a thing, inwardly swelling up, wholly bursts forth in itself, every part of itself in every other part, before it pours forth and boils over outwardly.

This explains the fact that the emanation of the persons in the Deity is the reason for creation and comes before it, for we read in John 1: "In the beginning was the word," and afterward: "All things were made through him."[12]

8 See above, p. 78.

9 Avicenna, *Metaph.* VIII, c. 4, fol. 99ra. For the notion of *anitas* see M. T. d'Alverny, "Anniyya-Anitas," *Mélanges offerts à Etienne Gilson* (Toronto, Paris, 1959), 59-91.

10 *Liber XXIV Philosophorum*, prop. 1; ed. Cl. Baeumker, *Beiträge zur Geschichte der Philosophie des Mittelalters*, 25, 1/2 (Münster i. W., 1927), p. 208.

11 John 1, 4.

12 John 1, 1, 3.

Again, the statement "I am who am" has the meaning Augustine gives it in his book *On the Trinity* VIII, 3, when he says: "God is not a good spirit or a good angel or a good heaven but a good Good."[13] And further on he says: "When you hear of this or that good, ... if you can abstract from them and perceive the good in itself, then you will have seen God." And further on: "He is nothing else but the Good itself, and consequently also the highest Good." The "good Good" therefore means the pure and supreme good which is rooted in itself, depends on nothing, and "returns full circle upon itself."[14] Thus the words "I am who am" signify the purity and fullness of existence, as we said above.

The fourth point to remark is that the word 'who' may sometimes by extending its meaning be used to inquire after a person's name, as Priscian points out in his small work, citing the verse of the poet:[15] "Who, father, is the man who thus attends him on his way?" It may even inquire after some other accidental circumstance, as in the words of John 1: "Who are you?"[16] and the like. But in the proper sense 'who', like 'what' inquires after the quiddity or essence of a thing,[17] which its name signifies and its concept or definition indicates.[18] Consequently, because in every creature existence and essence are distinct, the former being derived from something else and the

13 Augustine, *De Trinitate*, VIII, c. 3, n. 4; CCL 50 (Turnholt, 1968), p. 272, lines 24-25; p. 273, lines 46-52; p. 274, lines 61-62.

14 *Liber de Causis*, prop. 14; ed. O. Bardenhewer (Freiburg, Switz., 1882), p. 177.

15 Priscian, *Instit. gram.*, XVII, c. 3, n. 24; II, p. 123, lines 1-5. In the Middle Ages this work was divided into two parts, a 'larger part' containing books I-XVI, and a 'smaller part' containing books XVII and XVIII. See Virgil, *Aeneid*, VI, 864.

16 John 1, 19.

17 Prisican, *Instit. gram.*, XVII, c. 5, n. 37; II, p. 131, lines 8-10.

18 Aristotle, *Metaph.*, IV, 7, 1012a 23.

latter not being derived from anything,[19] the question whether a thing is is different from the question what a thing is, the former inquiring about the *anitas* or existence of the thing, the latter asking about its quiddity or essence, as we have said. Thus, if one asks "What is man?" or "What is an angel?" it would be foolish to answer "He is," or that the man or angel exists. But in the case of God, whose *anitas* is his quiddity itself, the fitting answer to the question "Who or what is God?" is simply "God is," for God's existence is his quiddity. "I am," he said, "who am." Pertinent to this is Augustine's statement in his book *On the Trinity* VIII, 2: "When you hear that he is truth, do not ask, what is truth?" [20] Further on he says: "Therefore remain, if you can, in that first flash in which you were dazzled as it were by its brightness, when it was said to you 'truth'." Bernard writes as follows in the fifth Book of his *On Consideration*: "If you say of God that he is good, great, blessed, wise, or any such thing, it is all summed up in this one word 'is'. For him the fact of existing is the same as being all these things."[21] He goes on to say: "This being, so unique and supreme — compared with it should not everything else be regarded as non-being rather than being?" This, then, is the meaning of the words "I am who am."

In the fifth place it should be noticed that when Rabbi Moses treats of the phrase "I am who am" in Book I, chapter 65, he apparently believes that it is the name 'Tetragrammaton', or at

19 This proposition was condemned at Cologne. See G. Théry, "Edition critique des pièces relatives au procès d'Eckhart," p. 176, n. 11, and Eckhart's reply, p. 195, n. 11. Eckhart appeals to both Avicenna and St. Albert for the truth of this proposition. See Avicenna, *Metaph.* V, c. 1, fol. 87r; St. Albert, *In I Librum de Causis*, c. 8, *Opera Omnia* X (Paris, 1891), p. 377.

20 St. Augustine, *De Trinitate*, VIII, c. 2; p. 271, lines 30-35.

21 St. Bernard, *De Consideratione*, V, c. 6, n. 13; PL 182, 795-796; *S. Bernardi Opera*, ed. J. Leclercq (Rome, 1963) III, p. 477, lines 13-15.

least close to that name which is "sacred" and "apart," "which is written and not pronounced," and which alone "signifies the creator's naked and pure substance."[22] I have commented on this name below in treating of the words "You shall not take the name of your God in vain." [23] Rabbi Moses means that the first 'I am' indicates the thing's essence and is the subject or thing denominated. The second or repeated 'I am' signifies existence and is the predicate or the denominator or denomination. Now it is generally the case that the thing denominated or the subject of the proposition is incomplete. The subject, as its name indicates, is incomplete, like matter. This is why Boethius says that "a simple form cannot be a subject."[24] But the denominator and denomination always function as the form and completion of the subject, as when someone is called just, good, wise, and the like, in which cases the essence is not self-sufficient but is needy and indigent, requiring something else to complete it.

This characteristic of needing something else and lacking self-sufficiency is wholly foreign to the essence of God, for "the first being is rich in itself."[25] So when he says "I am who am," he

22 Maimonides, *Dux seu Director Dubitantium aut Perplexorum*, I, c. 62 (Leipzig, 1522), fol. 26r 11 ff. On the sacred Tetragrammaton, see W. F. Albright, *From the Stone Age to Christianity*, 2nd ed. (New York, 1957), pp. 257-272; also works cited above in Introduction, note 36. See also A. Maurer, "St. Thomas on the Sacred Name 'Tetragrammaton'," *Mediaeval Studies* 34 (1972), 275-286.

The four letters of the Tetragrammaton (YHWH) are similar to those of the Hebrew 'I am'. Eckhart explains that 'Tetragrammaton', which means 'a name of four letters' is not itself the divine name. It is a circumlocution for the name of God, which is a holy secret and is inexpressible, like the divine substance itself. See Eckhart, *In Librum Exodi*, *LW* II, p. 131, n. 146.

23 See *ibid.*, p. 130, nn. 146-148. For the meaning of this name Eckhart refers not only to Maimonides but also to St. Thomas, *Summa Theol.* I, 13, 9 and 11. Here Eckhart, following St. Thomas, considers the Tetragrammaton to be a different divine name from 'He who is'. See *ibid.*, p. 142, n. 161.

24 Boethius, *De Trinitate*, c. 2; PL 64, 1250. *The Theological Tractates*, ed. H. F. Stewart and E. K. Rand (London, 1953), p. 10, line 43.

25 *Liber de Causis*, prop. 20, p. 182, line 16.

teaches that the subject 'I am' is the predicate, the second 'am', and that the denominator is the thing denominated, its essence its existence, its quiddity its *anitas*, and that "the essence is self-sufficient,"[26] and is sufficiency itself. In other words "it does not need the essence of any being, nor does it require anything outside itself to establish" – or complete — "it, but the essence is sufficient in itself" for everything and in all respects. Such a sufficiency belongs to God alone. In everything beneath God the essence is not self-sufficient for everything and in all respects. For example, the nature of a workman is not sufficient for him to practise his skill unless there is added the will to work, energy, knowledge, and the like, which are not identical with the nature of the workman. Hence in everything below God substance differs from power, existence, and operation. Such self-sufficiency on the part of God, therefore, is indicated when the words "I am who am" come forth from the person of God — 'I', as we have said, being used in the discrete sense. In support of this is the statement of Rabbi Moses in Book I, chapter 62, that "the two-letter name, taken from the Tetragrammaton, indicates the stability of the essence, and *Shaday* is derived from *day*, which means sufficiency."[27]

It must be noted, accordingly, that if the essence of anything — a man, for example — that which he is, were his existence, he would be a necessary being. "Nothing abandons itself," nor can it abandon itself, as Augustine says in his book *On the Immortality of the Soul*,[28] and nothing flees from itself, as he remarks in his *Book of Eighty Three Questions*.[29] The man in the above example would therefore be everlasting, always

26 Maimonides, *Dux seu Director Dubitantium aut Perplexorum*, I, c. 62, fol. 26r 9 ff.
27 *Ibid.*, lines 6-8.
28 St. Augustine, *De Immortalitate Animae*, c. 8, n. 15; PL 32, 1028.
29 St. Augustine, *Liber 83 Quaestionum*, c. 33; PL 40, 22.

lasting.[30] It would be impossible for him not to exist, and he would be a necessary being. Now God is his own existence. He is 'He who is', as it is said in this verse: "I am who am; He who is sent me." Therefore he is necessary being. Avicenna in his *Metaphysics* usually calls God necessary being.[31] Now existence itself stands in need of nothing, for it lacks nothing, whereas everything else needs it, because outside of it there is nothing. Nothingness stands in need of existence, as a sick man lacks health and is in need. Health has no need of a sick man. To be without the sick, not to have sickness, is perfect health. To want nothing, therefore, characterizes the highest perfection, is fullest and purest existence. And if existence is complete, it is accordingly life and wisdom, and so with every other perfection.[32] For just as he exists for himself and for all things, so also he suffices for himself and for all things: he is his own sufficiency and that of all things. As we read in 2 Corinthians 3: "Our sufficiency is from God."[33] God is not in want of existence, therefore, since he is existence itself. He is not in want of wisdom or power or the addition of any other perfection or extraneous thing. On the contrary, every perfection stands in need of him who is existence itself, both because each of them in and of itself is essentially a mode of existence resting upon and inhering in existence, and also because without existence it would be nothing, and would not be wisdom nor anything else but pure nothing. "Without him nothing was made," according to John 1[34] — as though to say: even "that which was made" which has and receives existence, such as wisdom and the like, without existence is simply nothing.

30 Eckhart is playing on the words *sempiternus, semper aeternus.*

31 Avicenna, *Metaph.* VIII, c. 1, fol. 97va2; c. 4, 98vb57, etc.

32 See St. Anselm, *Monologion*, c. 5. *Opera Omnia* I (Seckau, 1938), pp. 28-29. *Proslogion*, c. 12, p. 110, lines 6-8, c. 18, p. 114, lines 14-16.

33 2 Cor. 3, 5.

34 John 1, 3.

BIBLIOGRAPHY

Editions

Meister Eckhart. Die deutschen und lateinischen Werke (Stuttgart-Berlin, 1936-). Latin works, ed. J. Kóch et al., vol. 1-4 (1936-61), v. 56 (in progress). German works, ed. J. Quint, v. 1 (1936-58), v. 5 (1954-62), v. 2-4 (in progress). This edition supersedes all previous editions of Eckhart's works.

Magistri Eckhardi Opera Latina (Leipzig, 1934-36). Fasc. 1 *Super oratione dominica*, ed. R. Klibansky (Leipzig, 1934). Fasc. 2 *Opus Tripartitum, prologi*, ed. H. Bascour (Leipzig, 1935). Fasc. 13 *Quaestiones Parisienses*, ed. A. Dondaine (Leipzig, 1936).

Magistri Eckardi Quaestiones et Sermo Parisienses, ed. B. Geyer (Bonn, 1931).

Pfeiffer F., *Deutsche Mystiker des XIV. Jahrhunderts*, II, *Meister Eckhart* (Göttingen, 1924). English transl. by C. de B. Evans (London, 1924).

Quint, J., Meister Eckehart, *Deutsche Predigten und Traktate* (Munich, 1955). Latest translation into modern German of Eckhart's sermons and treatises.

Théry, G., "Le Commentaire de Maître Eckhart sur le livre de la Sagesse," *Archives d'histoire doctrinale et littéraire du moyen âge*, 3 (1928), 321-443; 4 (1929), 233-392.

Condemnation and Defense

Daniels, A., "Eine lateinische Rechtfertigungsschrift des Meister Eckhart," *Beiträge zur Geschichte der Philosophie und Theologie des Mittelalters*, XXIII, Heft 5 (Münster, i. W., 1923).

Denifle, H. S., "Aktenstücke zu Meister Eckeharts Prozess," *Zeitschrift für deutsches Altertum*, XXIX (1885), 259-66.

Laurent, M. H., "Autour du procès de Maître Eckhart. Les documents des Archives Vaticanes," *Divus Thomas* (Piacenza), series III, annus XIII (1936), 331-48, 430-47.

PELSTER, Fr., "Ein Gutachten aus dem Eckehart-Prozess in Avignon," *Aus der Geisteswelt des Mittelalters*. Festgabe M. GRABMANN (Münster i. W., 1935), 1099-1124. (Beiträge Supplement, III).

THÉRY, G., "Edition critique des pièces relatives au procès d'Eckhart contenues dans le manuscrit 33b de la bibliothèque de Soest," *Archives d'histoire doctrinale et littéraire du moyen âge*, I (1926), 129-268.

English Translations

BLAKNEY, Raymond Bernard, *Meister Eckhart. A Modern Translation* (New York and London, 1941). Contains: Talks of Instruction, The Book of Divine Comfort, The Aristocrat, About Disinterest, numerous Sermons, and the Defense.

CLARK, James M. and SKINNER, John V., *Meister Eckhart. Selected Treatises and Sermons*, transl. from Latin and German with an Introduction and Notes (London, 1958).

CLARK, James M., *Meister Eckhart. An Introduction to the Study of his Works, with an Anthology of his Sermons* (London, etc. 1957).

PFEIFFER, F. *Meister Eckhart*, transl. by C. DE B. EVANS, 2 vols. (London, 1924, 1931). Contains sermons and treatises.

Studies

ANCELET-HUSTACHE, Jeanne, *Master Eckhart and the Rhineland Mystics*, transl. by Hilda GRAEF (New York, 1957).

BANGE, Wilhelm, *Meister Eckeharts Lehre vom göttlichen und geschöpflichen Sein* (Limburg an der Lahn, 1937).

CLARK, James M., *The Great German Mystics, Eckhart, Tauler, and Suso* (Oxford, 1949).

HOF, Hans, *Scintilla Animae. Eine Studie zu einem Grundbegriff in Meister Eckeharts Philosophie* (Lund und Bonn, 1952).

KOCH, Josef, "Zur Analogielehre Meister Eckharts," *Mélanges offerts à Etienne Gilson* (Toronto-Paris, 1959), 327-350.

Lossky, Vladimir, *Théologie négative et connaissance de Dieu chez Maître Eckhart* (Paris, 1960).

Muller-Thym, Bernard, *The Establishment of the University of Being in the Doctrine of Meister Eckhart of Hochheim* (New York, 1939).

Shürmann, Reiner, *Maître Eckhart ou la joie errante. Sermons allemands traduits et commentés* (Paris, 1972).

The following histories of mediaeval philosophy contain brief accounts of Eckhart's thought.

Copleston, Frederick, *A History of Philosophy*, vol. 3, part 1 (New York, 1963), pp. 196-207. *A History of Medieval Philosophy* (London, 1972), pp. 279-285.

Gilson, Etienne, *History of Christian Philosophy in the Middle Ages* (New York, 1955), pp. 438-442.

Maurer, Armand, *Medieval Philosophy* (New York, 1962), pp. 292-303.

INDEX